Praise for *A Life i*

"[A] gentle but radiant me

"Her relationship to the pl........

and unflinching memoir." —*Psychotherapy Networker*

"Radiant essays about how joy and loss often coexist . . . To nudge readers toward building their own 'transcendent narratives,' Pipher braids in insights from her 25 years as a therapist, citing how acknowledging 'evidence of growth' in one's story, regardless of how big or small, can open up pathways toward healing. Those struggling to overcome darkness will find a guiding light in this incandescent work." —*Publishers Weekly* (starred review)

"A life story but also an homage to light . . . A beautifully written, quiet, contemplative memoir that many will enjoy." —*Library Journal*

"For psychologist Pipher, the light found in nature, caring relationships, work, and books has always been the key to happiness. In this beautifully written memoir, her memories of childhood in Nebraska are vivid and poignant . . . This lovely book teaches gentle lessons on gratitude and celebrating life." —*Booklist* (starred review)

"With a nod to her Buddhist practice and, amid climate change, to the passing away of the world as we've known it, Mary Pipher describes experiencing light of all kinds—literal and metaphorical. In *A Life in Light: Meditations on Impermanence.* Pipher tells a story of sorrow and loss in which she has nevertheless experienced much joy, love, and worldly success." —*Lion's Roar*

"In her incandescent new book, Mary Pipher shines a light on what really matters, and in doing so, she reflects our lives back at us with exquisite awareness. I was deeply moved by every page, laughing, crying, always reflecting on her words long after. She has given us all essential lessons on how to balance despair with a sense of wonder and inspires us to lead more light-filled lives." —Lori Gottlieb, *New York Times* bestselling author of *Maybe You Should Talk to Someone*

"Mary Pipher's work, always illuminating, is especially so in this dazzling memoir with its focus on light and transcendence. Beautifully written, heartfelt, and poignant, the book draws universal lessons from the rich details of Mary's life. Her luminous spirit shines on every page." —Jean Kilbourne, senior scholar, Wellesley Centers for Women, and author, cultural theorist, and filmmaker

"Mary Pipher transforms her own turning points into life lessons that illuminate purpose, intention, and joy for all her readers." —Jane Isay, author of *Unconditional Love*

"Profound insight, unflinching honesty, and deep compassion." —Gretchen Rubin

"Mary Pipher is a beacon, a light-bearer, a bodhisattva. Her life stories illuminate ways to be calm, connected, resilient, and joyful, regardless of circumstances. *A Life in Light* offers hope and direction while nurturing the heart and soul, mind and spirit." —Lama Surya Das, bestselling author of *Awakening the Buddha Within*

"William Blake says good is only found 'in the minute particulars,' and Mary Pipher here honors the particular beauty of memory, heartbreaking and heartwarming, with a tender presence and a lifelong opening to the light." —Jack Kornfield, author of *A Path with Heart*

Praise for *Women Rowing North*

New York Times Bestseller ★ *USA Today* Bestseller
Los Angeles Times Bestseller ★ *Publishers Weekly* Bestseller

"An enlightening look at how women can age joyfully." —*People*

"Both practical and inspiring." —*The New York Times Book Review*, "Inside the List"

"[Pipher's] 'quest for joy and happiness' is sincere, as is her commitment to helping other women achieve theirs. Some readers will treasure the book. All readers will admire her unadorned but wise summation that answered prayers are 'a surcease of worry.'" —*The Washington Post*

"Full of first-hand anecdotes, the hopeful book doesn't shield the reader from the realities of aging, but rather delivers thoughtful insight and guidance to help women get more out of their lives and to be happier. This mental makeover is a necessity when you consider our senior population, especially women, is growing faster than you can say 70 is new 60." —*Postmedia*

"Pipher offers warm, empathetic guidelines for navigating aging and for recognizing its unexpected gifts." —*BookPage*

"A wisdom-filled guide . . . Pipher's mindful tips act as a map to joy and remind us that we can flourish through *all* of our years" —*Woman's World*

"This is bound to become the bible of baby boomer women." —*Library Journal*, "Editors' Picks"

"Women of all ages will find much to reflect on, and respond to, in this collection of lives lived and lost." —NPR.org, "Best Books of the Year"

"Think of *Women Rowing North* as a GPS for navigating your later years. And while Pipher, 71, says she wrote it specifically for women crossing from middle age to old age, there is much in the book that is useful for any of us." —*Considerable*

"A work chock-full of wisdom and consoling messages . . . While a must-read for its target audience of women moving into old age, Pipher's engaging book is an ought-to-read for their daughters and sons as well, as it sets forth the universal message that 'happiness is a choice and a set of skills.'" —*Publishers Weekly* (starred review)

"Uplifting and calming . . . Pipher's skill of listening to clients and parsing meaning is evident in this volume filled with stories of women in the throes of change." —*Library Journal* (starred review)

"An encouraging, comforting and very welcome message about the strength and joy that can come with age." —AARP, "The Season's Big Books"

"Explores the stereotypes and challenges of getting older and the survival skills women need to be happy." —*The Wall Street Journal*

"This positive, affirming book will inspire and guide women facing these challenges." —*Booklist*

"Thoughtful, wise, and profoundly transformative, *Women Rowing North* tells the stories that make us feel accompanied and hopeful as well as providing models and muses for all the challenges and joys of this later stage of life. Pipher inspires us to take on this most important role, one that is most needed in challenging times of division and rancor: that of wise elders joining together and welcoming all into the beloved community she has labored to create. This is truly a one-of-a-kind book, one that I've been waiting for." —Julia Alvarez, author of *How the Garcia Girls Lost Their Accents* and *Once Upon a Quinceañera*

"In *Women Rowing North* Mary Pipher offers an illuminating, much-needed template for moving through advancing years with gratitude and grace—not through denial or rejection of what's broken and lost but by opening our hearts fully to everything our life delivers. This is a book to treasure, to keep by the bedside to remind us that, contrary to shopworn stereotypes, joy and wonder don't have a time stamp." —Barbara Graham, *New York Times* bestselling author of *Eye of My Heart*

"If I needed one book to guide me through the perils to the delights of aging, it is Mary Pipher's *Women Rowing North*. It sets the direction, shows the dangers, and brings the reader safely through to joy. I feel gratitude, not only for life, but for this wonderful book." —Jane Isay, author of *Unconditional Love*

"Simultaneously honest and calming, *Women Rowing North* is like an extended therapy session for millions of women who are strong and resourceful but need to be reminded of that. This book examines head-on the losses and crises we all fear, cohering into a profound and comforting guide to living deftly and deeply well into old age." —Meg Cox, author of *The Book of New Family Traditions*

"I love this book. Don't stop with a once-through reading. I myself keep it at hand to dip into for a quick shot of Mary Pipher's matter-of-fact wisdom, humor, and instinct for the essential. It never fails." —Joanna Macy, coauthor of *Coming Back to Life*

A Life in Light

A Life in Light

Meditations on Impermanence

MARY PIPHER

BLOOMSBURY PUBLISHING

NEW YORK · LONDON · OXFORD · NEW DELHI · SYDNEY

BLOOMSBURY PUBLISHING
Bloomsbury Publishing Inc.
1385 Broadway, New York, NY 10018, USA

BLOOMSBURY, BLOOMSBURY PUBLISHING, and the Diana logo
are trademarks of Bloomsbury Publishing Plc

First published in the United States 2022
This paperback edition published 2023

LIBRARY OF CONGRESS CATALOGING-IN-PUBLICATION DATA IS AVAILABLE

ISBN: HB: 978-1-63557-758-7; PB: 978-1-63973-163-3;
EBOOK: 978-1-63557-759-4

2 4 6 8 10 9 7 5 3 1

Typeset by Westchester Publishing Services
Printed and bound in the U.S.A.

To find out more about our authors and books visit
www.bloomsbury.com and sign up for our newsletters.

To Kate Elisabeth Pipher, who brightened the summer
of 2020 and who inspired this book; to Claire, a joyful
companion in the summer of 2021; to Aidan who stays in touch.
And to Coltrane and Otis, who still loved us when
we reunited in the fall of 2021.

CONTENTS

Introduction

Thomas A. Edison was born in 1847, and on October 21, 1879, he invented the incandescent light bulb. I was born on October 21, 1947, one hundred years after Edison's birth and on the sixty-eighth anniversary of his famous invention. By the time I discovered these facts, I was in my forties, but I had already developed a lifelong fascination with light.

Indeed, my first memory is of light dancing in the leaves of a tall tree in my grandmother's front yard in Sparta, Missouri. Aunt Grace had placed me on my back on a blanket under this tree. I remember the sunlight sparkling through the changing colors of the fluttering leaves and the occasional patch of cloud shadow that affected everything. I didn't have language, but I knew what I was watching was beautiful.

I remember nothing else about the first two years of my life, but I recall this as clearly as if it happened this morning. Light sticks in my memory that way. And ever since that seminal moment, dappled light has held the power to induce wonder in me.

I take note of shadows and sunspots and if a cloud crosses the sun. I stop to admire the sparkling dew on grass and flowers, the rainbows in lawn sprinklers, and the way certain kinds of light shine on birds' wings or breasts. I notice my cat glistening in the sunbeams and the way light sparkles on nearby Holmes Lake. These minute alterations in light affect me emotionally and even spiritually.

When I swim, the parabolas of light dancing on the bottom of the pool make me happy. So does the way sunlight splashing through rain can paint my porch with light. When I see shafts of sunlight breaking through storm clouds, I pay attention. When we travel, it is light that most astonishes me. Light in the Sandhills of Nebraska, in Alaska, in San Francisco, and in all the mountain towns along the front range of the Rockies.

As a college student and waitress, I avoided living in basement apartments. I cannot stay long in a room without a window, and, during the day, the shades are always up at my house. I would rather shovel horse manure outside than work in a cubicle or back room of a store.

I am solar-powered. As a child, I spent every waking moment outdoors in the summer. I spent my mornings mixing mud pies, cookies, and cakes on wooden slabs under an elm tree. And I spent long afternoons and evenings in our municipal pool. That's when I began reminding the other children to look at how sunlight twinkled on water.

I am fascinated by every kind of light—sunrise and sunset, light sparkling in fountains, and the light of celestial bodies. A prism anywhere makes my heart sing.

My memory is encoded by light. Whether I've been hunting for morels along the Platte or listening to my grandson Coltrane play music, I filter my experiences by quality of light. I can tell my story by simply remembering these lightscapes.

One of my favorite words is the Japanese word *komorebi*, which refers to the interplay of light and leaves as sunlight shines through trees. It has other meanings too. It can refer to a melancholic longing for a person, place, or thing that is far away. Or it can refer to impermanence. Dappled light shows us that what is here now will be gone in an instant. Nothing stays the same.

Resilience is the ability to find light in dark times. We build it by our attitudes, efforts, and coping skills. All of our lives we face crises that require us to grow. Struggle defines and builds us.

As a child, I worked hard to stay sunny. I looked for people to love me, and I basked in the nurturing relationships of those who did. I found solace in the natural world and in swimming. I discovered early the joys of hard work and of helping people and animals. The coping skills I learned as a child have stayed with me.

With each life stage, I have used them to stay calm and grounded.

All through my life, I've loved people and lost them. When I was a child, my father was off in the army in a faraway war. After he returned, I spent a year without my mother. In my twenties, my father died, and in my forties, my mother died. As I've grown older, I've had to say goodbye to many people I love.

When I wrote my last book, *Women Rowing North*, I was in full sunlight. My adult children and all five grand-children were nearby. I lived a life of travel, family, and friends. On weekends I danced to live music.

That brightness has faded. The young children who surrounded me have grown up or moved to Canada. And the pandemic has created painful separations for our family.

To be happy the last few years, I have needed to grow. I have utilized every skill I know to find the light. And I have learned to look inside myself for the love I cannot find in the world. I've developed new rituals and routines and now feel a renewed appreciation for life as it is, not as I wish it to be. If the first part of my life was about building attachments, the last two years have been about learning to detach. I am making an effort to find the love and warmth I need in my own heart.

No matter our age, we experience loss. A kindergart-ener must say goodbye to a beloved teacher at the end of the year. A pet dies. Or a grandparent. And every day we lose the world that was yesterday.

As we age, the losses multiply. We may no longer be in the workplace. Our friends and relatives move away or cross the River Styx. If we have children, they grow up and move on with their lives. We have no choice but to face impermanence.

The pandemic heightened our sense of isolation and loss, but these emotions are inevitable under any life circumstances. Eventually, one way or another, we all say goodbye to everyone we love. However, in the interim, we have the opportunity to grow our ability to find light within our own hearts and to orient toward the light of transcendence, which is finding joy and bliss in the midst of our pain. When we face loss, we can learn to experience wonder in order to restore our balance. There is a way to make this arithmetic work.

We can experience flashes of enlightenment. In the midst of ordinary life, a certain quality of light can transport me into bliss. My self dissolves into deep time.

Bliss is an absolute state. It can't be rated on a ten-point scale, and an experience can't be more or less blissful. If we are experiencing bliss, we are feeling the most wondrous possible experience. Over our lifetimes, if we grow in our capacity to live in the moment and pay attention, we may be fortunate enough to experience bliss more frequently. We may even have times in our life when we are showered with epiphanies. What was once an unusual experience may become an everyday one.

Komorebi describes our lives as we follow a path through a forest where the trees offer us both sunlight and shadow. Our journeys contain stories of loss and reunion, of despair and self-rescue. Most of us develop an identity that allows us to feel grateful in spite of our sorrows. We can feel a great sadness for our broken world yet still taste the spring strawberries or enjoy the smell of rain. Our hearts shatter into pieces, yet we hear the song of the cardinal and watch the exploding electricity of a thunderstorm.

This book describes my experiences with both literal and metaphorical light. As a therapist for twenty-five years, I helped clients build more transcendent narratives and progress on their journeys toward a luminous life. I now hope to do that for my readers as well.

As a therapist, I had several tools. One was predicting positive outcomes for clients, since we often find what we are looking for. Another was listening for evidence of growth. When I could find that, I underscored it so that clients could see they were moving toward light. No matter how painful their situations, I always asked clients two questions: *What did you learn from your experience? When you look back on this event, is there anything that you can feel proud of?*

This last question was particularly useful for people who had experienced trauma. It enabled them to move from a feeling of victimization to an awareness of their small acts of heroism, which I learned were always present.

I helped people create more empowering life stories. Without stories, we are without a self. With only stories of loss and sadness we are unhappy people. However, we can all learn to craft healing narratives. We humans are heliotropic. With a little guidance, most people can move toward more resilient, more connected, and more light-filled lives.

This trajectory is my hope for you. My story is really everyone's story. Yours will differ in its particulars, but the main themes of finding coping tools, appreciating beauty, and seeking transcendence are universal. We all must come to terms with impermanence and discover ways within ourselves to balance loss with joy. Let's explore this journey toward the light together.

I

Attachment and Loss

The Fountain

When I was five, my family was in a difficult situation. My father had signed up for the army just as the United States entered the Korean War. He had been home once in the three years since he had left in the fall of 1949. During that visit my mother had become pregnant with my brother John, who had yet to meet his father.

Occasionally our dad sent us presents from Korea. I received a cocoa cup he had decorated with raindrops and a pink umbrella. He had carefully printed my name on the side and at the bottom of the inside of the cup as a joke he had written STOP. He also sent me a doll and some bright Korean cloth. But really, we children had almost forgotten our father.

Mother's name was Avis, from the Latin root word for bird or soul. She was indeed soulful, although her singing voice was as croaky as a crow's. Our father was

Frank, appropriately named because a more authentic and direct man did not exist. I was the oldest of three. My brother Jake was one year younger, and my brother John was a baby. Our mother was in her third year of medical school and working long days. After putting us children to bed, she studied far into the night.

In a picture of her from that time, she is holding Jake and me on her lap, showing us a picture book. Jake is wearing a shirt so small for him that his entire belly is exposed. I am wearing a white T-shirt with the logo of Fitzsimons Army Hospital. Mother is in a cotton housedress with a flowered kerchief tied around her head. Her face is thin and she looks exhausted.

As our mother walked out the door early mornings, she would often say, "Be kind to each other." During the long days, we children were left with a series of house-keepers, none of whom could satisfy our mother's standards. She would deem the women she could afford to hire to be lazy or unclean and would soon fire them, only to hire an inept replacement. My brothers and I were free-range children living on a dirt road in a tiny house in what was then the small suburb of Aurora, Colorado.

From our relatives' stories, I ascertain that I was an early reader and that, even as a toddler, I could fall asleep only if I had a magazine or picture book to thumb through. I liked to ride my tricycle on the cracked side-walk and to play hide and seek with my brothers. Every night I waited on the stoop for my mother to come home, and, when she did, I barnacled myself to her side until bedtime.

Our mother was brave, unflappable, and endlessly patient. But her tasks were many and her free hours were few.

When our mother was with us, she was loving and attentive. She liked to bake and sew. Once, she made me a Lady Baltimore cake for my birthday. Sometimes she drove us into the mountains for picnics beside fast-moving, clear streams. We would take off our shoes and wade into those cold waters, walking gingerly on the sharp rocks and slipping and falling into the water, only to be carried a few feet downstream by the current. Chilly fun for all of us.

We could not afford most amusements, and the polio epidemic kept us out of public parks and away from large gatherings. On Saturday evenings we drove to the KOA radio station. We had discovered it by accident one night when our mother had taken us for a drive on the High Plains to see the stars. Jake noticed a tall lit tower and asked if we could go see it. When we arrived, we discovered something much better than the tower.

In front of the station was a large fountain illuminated by rotating colored lights of red, yellow, and blue. Our family would climb out of our car, sit on the warm hood of our Chevy, and watch the splashing colors change.

I remember everything about this experience—the heat of the day still emanating from the car hood, the cool breeze from the mountains, the sagebrush smell of the air, and the glittery stars above. But it was the fountain that entranced me, the way the light danced in the cascades of water and spray splashing red, then blue, then yellow, and of course the rainbow hues in between as it turned from one color to the next. Dazzled by the sparkling, colored lights, I forgot my missing father, my indifferent caregivers, my loneliness, and my restlessness.

At the time I didn't have words to explain my fascination, and I am not sure I have those words now, but this light on water was the most beautiful thing I had ever seen. I would stay focused on the fountain for a long time.

Of course, my little brothers quickly grew bored and ran around the parking lot. Our mother retired to the driver's seat and dozed. She was an expert on catnaps and would take them all her life.

Eventually, it would be time to climb back into the car for the ride home. I shut my eyes and would try to keep seeing those lights. Their beauty, the beauty of light, soothed me and carried me away from my everyday life into something vast and universal.

It still does.

A Motherless Child

The summer before I started first grade, my father returned from the Korean War. He rejoined a family that had long managed without him. My mother was absorbed in her medical studies and had her ways of doing things at home. We children hardly knew our dad and were not eager to bond with a man who might be leaving us again soon.

By age six, I was old enough to observe how different my parents were. They were both smart, but in different ways. Mother was a hardworking scientist, steady and serious, but stiff and awkward with people. She did not like us to touch her face or hair and was not a physically affectionate person. I believe now that she was on the autism spectrum, long before that category was known to exist. Dad was extroverted, impulsive, charming, and a big talker. He was chubby with jet-black curly hair, and he looked and acted a little like Jackie Gleason on the *Honeymooners*. He liked to say he worked to live and lived to play. He could create a party out of thin air.

He was always cooking up plans and trying something new. I remember people asking my dad, "Frank, where's the fire?" Or, "Do you ever sit down?"

When he reentered our family, he wasn't used to being a father. He had been living with army men who in their rare free hours drank, played cards, and explored local nightlife. As a medic at Incheon and the Chosin Reservoir, he had carried men off battlefields and patched them up. Some he had declared dead and collected their personal belongings to send home to the families.

The trauma of this brutal war was compounded by the trauma he had suffered during World War II, when he had been on a submarine in the South Pacific and a medic in Okinawa and the Philippines. My father had experienced too much killing, death, cruelty, and sorrow. And he lived in a time when men had neither the language nor the permission to discuss their emotions.

Of course, I didn't know about his suffering, and even my mother had never heard of PTSD. What I knew was that he could be grumpy and hot-tempered. He and my mother fought every evening, and he usually made her cry.

Jake, John, and I hadn't been exposed to shouting and cursing, and it scared us and left us unsettled. We couldn't predict what our dad would do next. In the space of ten minutes, he could make us all laugh or have us in tears.

After about a month of rather dreadful days, my dad announced that the family would be splitting up for a while. He would take my youngest brother John to live with our grandparents in eastern Colorado. Then he would drive Jake and me to a trailer just outside Sparta, Missouri, behind my Aunt Grace and Uncle Otis's house. This was where he had grown up and where most of his relatives still lived. My mother, who was newly pregnant, would stay in Denver to complete her internship year. Every night I knelt by my little bed and prayed that we wouldn't have to go. I begged my mother to let me stay with her, and she said sadly but firmly that it was impossible.

After that, my memories grow blurry. I don't remember leaving my mother or saying goodbye to my little brother, or the long drive from Colorado to southeastern Missouri, or reconnecting with relatives whom I had forgotten.

What I remember is the trailer, which was small and dark. It made me uneasy. We walked up three rickety steps into a small kitchen / living room area with two windows, a cereal-box-size one over the kitchen sink and a larger one over the orange couch in the living room. Just off this area was a small bathroom and a hall that led to a bedroom. The bottom bed was for my dad, and over his bed hung two shelves for Jake and me. The bedroom felt like a claustrophobic cave.

During the fall and spring, Jake and I could be outside, but in the winter and after dark we spent almost all our time inside the trailer. I developed a physiological and psychological response to this that I called *squishy*. This word to me meant that my stomach was upset, my mouth was dry, and I felt sad, confused, and not quite in my body.

Our father was rarely there, and mostly Jake and I just lay on our beds and slept or talked. Our life force was weak. Or perhaps I should say we were hibernating.

Some nights our father came home and made us dinner or brought us groceries, but other nights he stayed late in Springfield, where he was going to school on the GI Bill. When he finally arrived home, Jake and I trundled out of our beds, hungry and dazed. Sometimes he brought us food, sometimes he didn't.

Even as I describe what we would now call neglect, I feel the need to defend my father. That year he was holding on for his own dear life and trying to deal with his war trauma in the only way he knew to do it, by drinking and running around with his buddies. He had almost no understanding or empathy for the needs of children. He didn't even understand himself. If he could have done better, he would have. I loved my dad, and, in spite of his lack of responsibility that year, I knew he was a good and heroic man. Just not all the time.

On weekends, he would take us to visit his sister Henrietta's family. Her son Steve, who was six years older than me, became our best friend that year. Steve was a skinny kid with a crew cut, a shy smile, and a laconic personality. His soft voice and accommodating manner helped calm Jake and me. Steve told us jokes, took us fishing, and listened to our ideas. I remember one afternoon when the three of us sat in a mulberry tree eating berries. Jake and I poured all our miseries out to him. Steve just handed us more berries and said, "Things will get better." And, "You are going to be okay."

Sometimes, Dad drove us to Grandma Glessie's house. She loved us up and fixed us big meals, always with biscuits and gravy. Glessie and Dad would drink coffee, smoke, and talk far into the night. Jake and I could walk to downtown Sparta and look in the store windows or buy a candy bar or can of pop at the gas station on the highway.

My great-grandmother Granny Lee, Glessie's mother who lived with her, suffered from rheumatoid arthritis. She never left her daybed in the windowless living room of Glessie's tiny house. Jake and I didn't care for Granny Lee because she was always ordering us about and shouting if we didn't please her. Mostly we stayed in the bright kitchen with its wood stove, big table, and pump from the outdoor cistern.

Every weekday morning, Jake and I rode to school on a bus that stopped in front of Uncle Otis's mailbox down by the road. We wore ragged, ill-fitting clothes and had meager social skills to match. I liked school with all its bright colors, books, and activities. My classroom had a piano, and one day a little boy and I played a duet of Chopsticks. Afterward he gave me a kiss on the cheek. That made me happy and excited. He was a sweet boy, shy and polite. I thought I had a boyfriend, although I didn't even know what that meant. But I knew I had a tender friend who would smile at me when I walked into the classroom.

Another day my class rode the bus to Sedalia for the state fair. I had a dollar to spend, but I held my dollar out the window and it blew away. I cried and my teacher gave me another dollar. This kind teacher, who no doubt understood I was struggling with a difficult home life, probably didn't have many dollars to spare.

After school, Jake and I would walk into the dark, messy trailer and wait for our father to come home. One night, we were out of groceries and he didn't return. Resigned to our fate, we lay, stomachs growling, in our bedroom cave. Just as we were falling asleep, Aunt Grace knocked on our door and invited us over. We walked across the dark lawn into her kitchen for a meal. Her family had eaten, but she piled our plates high with fried chicken, biscuits, mashed potatoes, and green beans with bacon. The food tasted delicious, and we ate like the famished children we were.

What I most remember about that night was the brightness of Grace's kitchen. Her floor was tiled in cherry red, and, instead of a dinner table, the family had a shiny yellow leatherette booth. Everything was sparkly, and the electric lights made the room look radiant. I am sure Aunt Grace asked us over other times, but I remember this one special night, when we felt saved by the yellow booth, Mr. Edison's lights, and fried chicken.

In the summer, Dad took Jake and me fishing, mushroom hunting, or visiting his pals who were scattered all over Christian County. Sometimes he drove us to a rocky ford on the James River, and we would hunt for crawdads while he washed his car.

On one of those occasions, Jake and I were swarmed by leeches. When we got out of the water, our legs and bellies were covered by what looked like giant purple grapes. We asked our dad what they were, and when he told us, we started screaming. I screamed the loudest and begged to be helped first. He removed them one by one by holding his cigarette lighter up to them until they fell off. It was a gruesome experience, but Dad was calm and steady.

We didn't have a telephone in the trailer. I assume that my mother wrote my dad and also us children letters, but I don't remember this. I have no recall of Christmas or any other holidays that long year. Our relatives were kind to us, but most of them had busy, complicated lives of their own. The best thing I can say about that year is that it came to an end.

That year without my mom has shaped my life. Ever since then, I can't stand enclosed or dark places, I have anxiety attacks in trailers, and I wilt when I am not in contact with family or people I love. When I am reexperiencing that earlier trauma, I again feel "squishy."

That year without my mother was mostly shadow, but light arrived in the form of a kind teacher, my calm and steadfast Cousin Steve in the dappled light of the mulberry tree, the yellow booth in Aunt Grace's kitchen, and Grandma Glessie's expansive love. That year taught me one of the tricks about staying alive: always finding the light.

Golden Light

In June, just after school was out, my father told us we were rejoining our mother, brother John, and new sister Toni. I remember the morning, a spring Saturday. Jake and I headed through the meadow to Uncle Otis's farm pond. The dew sparkled on the purple clover and the blue flax. Spiderwebs turned into kaleidoscopes in the sunlight. Birds seemed to be singing with the same high spirits that I felt. Jake and I were twirling and shouting for joy. Soon we would see our family. We had a new baby sister. I felt as if I were awakening from a nightmare into the dawn of a fresh, bright day.

A few days later, Dad, Jake, and I drove the six hours from the Ozarks to a small town in Kansas where we would meet up with our family. Then all of us would caravan to Dorchester, Nebraska, where Mother would start her first medical practice.

Dad, Jake, and I arrived after dark when all the stores had closed in the town. Dad parked on the quiet main street and lit a smoke. Jake and I were hungry, but we didn't much care. We were used to it, and besides, we were waiting for our mother. We sat quietly in the back seat. As I watched the red tip of my father's cigarette, I fell asleep.

The next thing I remember is my mother tapping me on the shoulder and saying, "Mary, I am back."

As I embraced her, I felt infused with warmth. A heat lamp had been turned on inside me. What had been frozen for a year began to melt.

Seeing my mother and brother again was more than a reunion with beloveds. It was my own awakening after a year of hibernation. I had stopped growing physically that year, and I had slept as much as I could. But now, I was out of the cave and on my way to someplace better.

I even had a baby sister who had been living with my Aunt Agnes since her birth. My mother had picked Toni up in Flagler along with our brother John. Toni was almost three months old, with gray eyes and white-blond hair. She curled her hand around my thumb and pulled it toward her face. She was a pretty baby, but my attention was focused on Mother.

I knew I would be joyous on seeing my mother, but I didn't anticipate the two of us being enfolded by golden light in the back seat of our old car. This is not a metaphor. The light was visible, as real as my mother herself. I felt this light inside and outside my body.

This golden light stayed with us while we held each other. It haloed half the back seat, and I was conscious of its presence alongside my joy in a way that I could neither understand nor describe. I didn't know that this golden light would return in my life many times over.

That night I thought I had survived the hardest thing possible. But I was only six, and there were some surprises ahead.

My Father's Shirt

Dorchester, Nebraska, was a town of four hundred inhabitants, most of whom were Czech. The Mariskas, Hrdvas, Walenchenskys, and Dzerks were my mother's patients and my second-grade schoolmates. In my class, the four other girls were two sets of cousins, and all of them spoke Czech at recess. My brothers and I played alone in the schoolyard.

That year we had a housekeeper who took care of Toni and baked us cinnamon rolls and pie. I saw my parents every day and was happy to once again be with John. The teachers let me borrow all the books that I wanted, and I inhaled *Heidi, the Bobbsey Twins series, Five Little Peppers and How They Grew,* and *Little House on the Prairie.*

One day I came home from school early with a bad stomachache. Our housekeeper sent me to my mother's office for a checkup. My mother felt my stomach, drew some blood, and quickly diagnosed appendicitis. After work she drove me to the nearby hospital in Crete.

I had never before been a patient and was quite frightened by it. Because my mother had privileges at the hospital, admittance was quick and I was soon in bed in a big white room. There was a window, but the shade was drawn and the room felt dusky even with the light on. A nurse came by for a urine sample and another blood draw.

My mother was called to an emergency at her clinic. She kissed me goodbye and said she would see me in the morning after my surgery. She told me to be a brave girl and do what the doctor and nurses asked me to do.

Without Mother and alone with my thoughts of the next day, I panicked. All I really knew about surgery is that doctors cut you open with a big knife, took out body parts, and sewed you back up. What a frightening set of images for an eight-year-old with a runaway imagination.

I didn't have any books with me, and this was before television or cell phones. I was alone with my racing thoughts and my stomachache.

Eventually a nurse came in to tell me it was bedtime and that she wanted to give me a shot to put me to sleep. Suddenly, I thought of animals being "put to sleep." I knew the nurse wasn't planning to kill me, but I quite rightly suspected this was the beginning of a process in which I would be knocked out, rolled into a surgery room almost naked, and cut open by a big knife. Perhaps if I had been with one of my parents I could have been calmed down, but as it was, I was terrified.

I looked into the nurse's eyes and said, "No, you can't give me that shot."

She raised her eyebrows in surprise and moved toward me, but I pushed her away. She tried reassuring and cajoling me to be a big girl, but I wasn't having it.

"No. No. No," I said. I was shaking, but I was adamant.

The nurse left and returned with a doctor who worked with my mother. I didn't know him well, but he greeted me pleasantly.

"Young lady," he said, "what's this I hear about you refusing a shot?"

I started trembling, but I once again said I would not allow that shot. The doctor's face reddened and his jaw tightened. He announced, "I am going to administer this medication. Nurse, hold her down."

Somehow the two of them wrestled me into a helpless position, but as the doctor moved in with the syringe, frightened animal that I was, I bit his arm.

He yelped in surprise, and then he plunged in the needle.

My body went limp and I flopped down onto the bed. Slowly, I realized what I had done. I could hardly believe it. I was the most docile of children and had never even wanted to hurt a bug. I buried my head in the pillow so the doctor couldn't see me cry.

The doctor's voice was hoarse with anger, and, as he left the room, he said, "I am going to tell your mother about this episode."

The next morning, I woke up when a nurse came in to take my pulse and temperature. I asked her what day it was.

She responded, "It's Thursday and your surgery went fine. Stay in bed until we have time to help you up."

After she left, I fell back to sleep. The next time I woke up, my whole family had crowded into the room. Toni was a smiling baby in mom's arms. John was sucking his thumb and had his T-shirt on backward. Bony, skinny Jake just smirked with happiness seeing that I was okay.

The nurse had drawn up the window shade, and the room was flooded with light. That day my father had a white shirt on, and it gleamed in the sunlight. Just gleamed.

He passed around a box of grape Popsicles and told me I could have one. My brothers gave me grapey pecks on the cheek. As I licked my delicious Popsicle, my father told jokes and we all laughed. It hurt to laugh, and, after the first joke, I held my stomach.

My mother was wearing her white coat and stethoscope. She refused a Popsicle, but she watched us enjoy ours and she laughed at my dad. He could really be so funny.

After the others left, my mother said quietly, "The doctor told me that you bit him." She paused and shook her head. "Mary, I am disappointed in you."

I felt the shame burn through my body. I looked
down. No punishment could be harsher than those
words from my mother. When we had been separated
for a year, I was convinced that it was my fault, that I
must have done something terribly wrong to deserve
exile. Ever since, I had been fearful of making mistakes
or being a bad girl. Now that I had bitten a doctor, an
action much worse than anything I had ever done before,
part of me believed I would surely be exiled again.

Mother stood by the door in silence for what seemed
like a long time. I couldn't look at her. Finally, I heard
her high heels tap toward me. She came to my bedside
and gave me a quick kiss on the forehead. That was a rare
gesture for her, and I felt my tense body relax. She said,
"After work tonight, I will come and take you home."

II

Becoming

Light Filtered Through Water

The summer I finished fourth grade, we moved to Beaver City, Nebraska, where we lived in a green stucco house on the north edge of town. This house was small, and, when it was cold, I slept on a daybed in the living room. In the spring and summer, I slept on a cot outdoors on the wraparound porch.

I loved outdoor sleeping in the summer. At night I could hear coyotes calling and the hoots of great horned owls. Frogs croaked happily on nearby farm ponds, and crickets and cicadas sang from the pastures and fields. It was much cooler outside than inside. I could watch the trees sway in the wind and look at the stars.

Except for my father, everyone was happy with the move.

The Beaver City years were difficult for Dad. He was farther from his Ozark family and closer to my mother's. Her family disapproved of his swearing, drinking, and off-color jokes. They felt my mother was far superior to him in character and intellect. Also, Mother was the primary wage earner and the one with status in the community. This was the 1950s, and Dad felt ashamed of that. He vowed never to work at a hospital where my mother was on the staff, and, throughout his time as a lab technician, he would drive as far as a hundred miles from home to fulfill that vow.

Dad was unhappy with his wild, unkempt children, his absent wife, and his totally disorganized household. At this time he was working at a tuberculosis sanatorium twenty-five miles away in Norton, Kansas, and he slept there during the week. When he came home on weekends, he drank tequila, argued with our mother, and shouted at us kids. "What the goddamn hell have you been doing? Get your sorry asses out here and clean up this mess."

My friends told me they were afraid of him. He went easy on me, but he was hard on my brothers. Sometimes I stood between them and begged him to leave them alone. Sometimes that worked.

One night, while I was reading in the daybed, my parents were arguing in the kitchen. Dad was slurring his speech and not making much sense. He was near the stove, and Mother was across the room next to the refrigerator. He was shouting, and she was quietly defending herself. She never raised her voice to anyone.

As he became more and more agitated, I sensed my mother's fear. She had stopped moving or speaking. I felt my heart race and my face tighten up. Finally, Dad picked up a large cast-iron skillet and hurled it across the kitchen toward my mother. It whizzed by so close to her head that it ruffled her short hair. As the heavy skillet clattered to the floor, my parents looked at each other wide-eyed and speechless. We all knew he could have killed her. For a moment I felt as if we had been flash frozen. Nobody moved. Time stopped.

The realization of what had happened ended the argument. My dad left through the back door, and my mother finished cleaning the kitchen and went to bed. She never looked at me. She probably didn't know what to say, and so she said nothing. I lay awake in the dark for a long time, waiting for my body to defrost.

My salvation was the swimming pool, open from Memorial Day through Labor Day. In the mornings, my brothers and I took swimming lessons. Often the water was warm, but the air was cool. We shivered on the side of the pool as our teacher asked one student after another to demonstrate a crawl or backstroke. As the sun rose and we warmed up, the water shone royal blue. Later in the day, it was aquamarine, and at night, under the lights, it was robin's-egg blue shot through with beams of light.

Afternoons, my brothers and I were there when the doors opened, and we stayed until dinner. We kept our swimsuits on while we ate, and many nights, after refueling at home, we biked back to the pool to be there until it closed. And, as if that weren't enough time in the water, we fantasized about sneaking into the pool after-hours for a secret swim.

Every summer, I turned bronze and my long hair turned ivory-blonde. It also had greenish tints and was a little slimy from the chlorinous pool water.

In the afternoons, we kids practiced dives, played water tag, and had races. We organized hold-your-breath and floating contests. We talked as we treaded water. Occasionally we girls sunbathed while the boys showed off for our benefit, but mostly I was in the water.

Back then I didn't wear goggles. When I was under water, I sometimes opened my eyes and looked at the sky. The sunshine burst in on me like a hula-hoop-size sunflower. This bright-beyond-bright light induced a beauty trance in me. I felt a deep sense of love, safety, and well-being.

The sunlight and cool, clear water made me feel happy and hopeful. Swimming pumped vitality into me. Water was my healing elixir, my curative for sadness. The sunlight baked away my tears.

A Best Friend

Beaver City was a step up for me. I found kids to play with in our neighborhood. My friend Jeanie, daughter of our town newspaper's editor, lived a block away in a three-story house with a big veranda. Jeanie had a pug nose, tight red curls, and blue eyes that sparkled with mischief. I was a tall, angular kid, while Jeanie was short, soft, and curvy, but, in most ways, we were very much alike.

We were both outspoken and opinionated. Jeanie was quick-tempered and I was easily hurt, but when we argued, we made up quickly. We didn't want to waste our time doing anything that wasn't fun.

We often walked to the drugstore to buy gum. My favorite was Black Jack licorice, while Jeanie was a fan of bubble gum. I was not coordinated enough to blow bubbles and I admired her great skill. One memorable afternoon, she blew a bubble as big as her face. When it popped, she had gum in her hair, eyelashes, and ears. She had me take her picture, and later we laughed at the pink blob covering her features, surrounded by gummy curls.

Another time we found her dad's ancient bottle of Mogen David wine in the refrigerator. We poured ourselves small glasses and proceeded to act drunk, slurring our words, falling on the floor, and saying the stupidest things we could. We thought we were hilarious.

Jeanie was the better prankster, but I was the more skilled reader. We both started with the Dana Girls and Nancy Drew, but I quickly moved into history, auto-biography, and grown-up novels. By eighth grade I was reading the Russians. I gave her my copy of *Doctor Zhivago*, annotated just for her. I told her, "Don't let all the long Russian names and nicknames discourage you. This book is worth the effort."

We spent lots of time at Jeanie's, rocking on her wooden glider swing or lying in the grass, by day watching sunlight and clouds and at night finding the Big Dipper among the glittery stars. We counted falling stars and learned the names of the constellations.

In winter we lay on her lacy bedspread talking about school and outlining our dreams for the future. I wanted to live in New York City and work as an editor. Jeanie wanted to be a traveling nurse like Cherry Ames, the heroine of an adventure series for young girls.

One afternoon I told her I wished my mother would stay home like other mothers. I told her that at my house, no one was in charge. I felt too responsible for my younger siblings. I had never said that to anyone and I trembled as I talked. Jeanie didn't know what to say but she could listen.

Afterward, we both cried.

When younger people ask me for advice about having a happy life, I always say, "Surround yourself with good friends and keep them close." I have gone on to make many more friends over the course of my life. These friends have sustained me, given me joy, and helped define me. But at age nine, having a best friend and confidante changed my life. I learned to joke around and be irreverent, even slightly naughty. I still had my identity as the daughter of a doctor in an odd family, but I added a new identity. I was a girl with a friend.

Animal Companions

We children were allowed to have whatever pets we wanted. Our parents made decisions casually and quickly. Our mother did this because she was always in a hurry and preoccupied with work. Our father was impulsive and never worried about consequences. Their attitude toward pets was rather like their attitude toward children—just have some and see what happens.

At the state fair one year, Dad bought us chameleons. I was ignorant about zoology but eager to experiment. Right away I put my chameleon on my plaid jumper to see if it could turn red, green, black, and white all at once. Sadly, it couldn't. I also tried to turn this overworked chameleon pink, blue, and purple. To my disappointment, her coloration range was from brown-green to green-brown.

On the way home from Padre Island, Texas, one year, Dad impulsively had stopped in Dallas and purchased a Chihuahua. Her name was Pixie Rosarita, and she was a wonderful friend, although barky and with long toenails that drew blood. Pixie adored me, and the feeling was mutual. I loved her wet, black eyes always trained on me. I liked to run my fingers through her short Brillo-pad coat. Almost everywhere I walked, Pixie tapped along beside me. Even when I rode a bike, Pixie tried hard to keep up but, with her short little legs, she couldn't do it.

One summer, Dad bought me a blue parakeet I named Ernie and a green parakeet I named Eve. I enjoyed everything about those birds but cleaning their cages. Both of them would sit on my fingers and cock their little heads as I talked to them. But our house lacked central heating, and when winter came, the north-facing room where the birds lived was cold.

One January day after school, I walked into that bedroom to visit my birds. Ernie and Eve lay stiff as bricks on the cage floor. Their eyes were open, their wings at their sides, and their little toes were curled up under them. I held one in each hand and tried to warm them back to life. But I had arrived too late. I cried and cried in that cold room. Then Jake and I carried them outside and dug a hole in the hard ground and buried them.

Every spring, Dad bought a dozen rabbits and put them in cages in our old car shed by the alley. My brothers and I named them and played with them all summer. Bunnies are the cuddliest of animals, and they have the softest ears and the warmest eyes. We carried them to the yard and let them hop around eating grass and weeds. Late mornings before the pool opened, we snuggled with them in the shade.

Yet, every fall, our dad would remove them from their cages, hit them over the head with a hammer, hang them on a tree in our backyard and skin them. He'd clean them and freeze the meat. That first year I was emotionally unprepared for his actions.

I sobbed and screamed, but Dad had no patience with me. My brothers were upset too, but they had already learned not to cry. We pleaded with our dad to show the rabbits mercy, but he didn't listen to us.

He had almost starved as a child and didn't have the luxury of being soft-hearted about food supplies. He said, "You'd better toughen up if you want to be ready for the real world."

We kids were helpless to stop a six-foot-tall, determined man. However, when winter came, we refused to eat that rabbit meat.

Over the years, we ate all kinds of animals. My dad cooked the meat he had grown up eating—squirrel, rattlesnake, frog legs, and snapping turtle. He also prepared tripe soup, hominy and pigs feet, brains with scrambled eggs, tongue, sweetbreads, and mountain oysters. From his time in Japan and Korea during the war, he fixed us bulgogi, kimchi, sukiyaki, and yakitori.

People told us that every time they ate at our house they tasted something new.

Sixty years ago rural Nebraska was rich in wildlife. First, tadpoles filled the ditches, then frogs, whose croaking could be heard at dusk and dawn. At our doors in the spring, box elder bugs swarmed in such numbers that it was scary to walk through them. In June, rivers of lightning bugs flowed across our lawns and landed in our hair and on our clothes.

Driving on state highways or country roads, our windshield would soon be covered with dead insects. Every few minutes, tumbleweeds the size of bushel baskets blew across the road. Jackrabbits hopped in front of our car constantly, and when we went south to the Ozarks, turtles covered the highways. There were so many animals it was impossible not to hit a few, although at our insistence, Dad swerved to avoid them.

On the way home from the Ozarks, Dad would pull the car over and let us kids each pick out a turtle. We would bring them back to Nebraska as pets. One year we named them Achilles, Paris, Hector, and Anthony after a story of the Greeks our mother had told us. I can still picture my brothers barefoot with crew cuts, wearing dirty jeans and T-shirts as we crawled around on the grass following our turtles. We played with our turtles all summer, and then, when fall came, we pointed their heads south and released them.

Every spring, our neighbor Alvin Rogers searched for baby coyotes in the dens. He brought them home in bushel baskets, then killed them and carried their ears to the county agent. My brothers and I were often in the Rogerses' house because Alvin had a Down syndrome daughter who never left home. Our mother would send us over to visit Jolene several times a week. We would show her our latest baby chickens or take her a Fudgsicle.

One spring day when I was visiting, I heard some coyotes yipping and I headed for the sounds from the back porch. Alvin didn't want me to see them and tried to keep me off the porch, but I sprinted through the door ahead of him. Two bushel baskets full of wriggly coyote puppies sat by the back door. As I patted the pups and oohed and aahed about their cuteness, Alvin was uncharacteristically grumpy. I kept asking what he was doing with them, and, reluctantly, he told me that he sold their ears for bounty, a dollar a pair.

I was stunned and ran out of his house and back to our kitchen where my mother was making spaghetti sauce. I burst into tears as I told her about Alvin's plan. She said, "Mr. Rogers is a good man who needs the money." She gave my brothers and me each a dollar so that we could go save three pups.

My brothers and I looked down into the bushel baskets of pups crawling all over each other and yipping softly for their mothers. We had a hard time choosing, partly because we knew that the ones we didn't choose were doomed, but we each picked our pet and carried our wriggly new friend home.

The coyotes lived in our house all summer, going outside only when we took them out to play. They tore the stuffing out of the bottom of a mattress and slept there. We fed them hamburger and leftover meat from meals. They were great fun, but in autumn they started to get more aggressive. We carried them to Beaver Creek and let them go. We left them a pound of ground beef and hoped they could make it on their own.

I had plenty of time to wander around town and the nearby countryside. One spring afternoon as I walked home from school, I found a nest of baby squirrels in a gutter. All but two were still alive, and I decided to take the others home and save them. These were young squirrels, still naked and no bigger than my little finger, and the act of rescuing them made me excited and happy. I found a shoebox and filled it with soft cloth, then I dipped a piece of cotton in milk and let each baby suck on this cloth. I put my squirrels on a shelf by our heater and fed them almost every hour during the day.

From then on, I resolved to rescue every animal I could find.

On rainy and windy days, I would hunt for baby animals in ditches and gutters and under downed tree branches. I would bring them home to my little hospital with its shoeboxes and soft cloths. Over the years, I saved many a mouse, possum, squirrel, and bird. I fed tiny mammals sips of milk from a piece of cloth and kept baby birds alive by squirting thin oatmeal from a dropper into their mouths.

One of the birds, Maggie, turned into an elegant adult magpie who returned to our yard every summer and followed me when I biked to the pool. She would sit on the high fence and watch me and the other children swim, then follow me back home.

Even though most animals' eyes are dark brown or black, they sparkle with an unusual kind of light. On the rare occasions when wild animals look into our eyes, it is an immense gift—a wondrous moment that can feel as if we have made a deep and primal connection and have seen beyond our human boundary.

I've been lucky enough to make many eye-to-eye connections with wild animals—with deer in the Nebraska woodlands, with a coyote near Holmes Lake, and with a weasel in the Snowy Range of Wyoming. I was hiking back from searching for pretty rocks in a field of granite when I encountered the young weasel sitting bright-eyed on a big chunk of granite. I stopped, looked him in the eyes, and spoke softly to him. "How are you, little buddy? So nice to meet you. I've never met a weasel before."

He kept his eyes on me and switched his tail back and forth, but he wasn't afraid. He seemed as curious about me as I was about him. I continued, "I am having a good day, little friend. I hope you are too. Don't worry, I will leave soon."

I had planned to say more, but the weasel put his paw to his mouth and yawned. At that moment he looked so human that I burst into laughter. That startled him and our moment ended. But to this day I am the only person I know who has bored a weasel.

When I woke at dawn this morning, I saw the red fox on our driveway and heard the great horned owl who lives in our pines. As I write, I can see mourning doves and juncos on my porch, and my old calico Glessie purrs by my side. When she looks at me with her caramel-colored eyes, she reminds me that I am not alone.

The Library

Beaver City was large enough to have a luxury that Dorchester didn't—a small brick library located just off the town square. In five minutes, I could bike to it from my home.

Before Beaver City, I had never been inside a library. In my grandmother's town of Flagler, I had visited the bookmobile that came through town every Friday morning. We inched through the narrow little van to the two shelves that contained children's reading, and Grandmother helped me select a few books to enjoy during my visit.

Beaver City was blessed with a real library, solemn and quiet, with only soft footsteps and the occasional whisper. A bright white lamp lit the librarian's desk, and, in each aisle, a bare light bulb emitted just enough light to read the titles. Globe lamps on the reading tables spilled circles of lemony light.

Everything about the library seemed holy—the dim lighting, the silence, and the smells of leather, floor wax, and old paper. Its sanctified stations were clearly defined. Card catalogs crowned two wooden stands. Visitors stood before them and leafed through soft faded cards interspersed with a few fresh ones that signaled a new book or a popular older one. Pearl S. Buck's *The Good Earth* had one new card after another, as the women of our town checked it out as soon as it returned to the shelves.

The heavy wooden tables allowed us to sit side by side with our fellow citizens. The stacks, arranged by the Dewey Decimal System, made it easy to walk down the aisles, reading titles, pulling out books, and carrying them to the table for further perusal.

It was possible to spend half a day in the library, examining books or reading the newspapers from Omaha, Kansas City, and Denver. In a town with no television and few places to go, many people were readers, and the library could be busy on a rainy afternoon.

My favorite ritual was checking out books. The library card in its tan folder at the back of the book allowed me to see who else had read the book and how often it had been checked out since its purchase. I could examine everyone's signatures and then add my own loopy schoolgirl writing to the card.

The librarian, Mrs. Schaefer, was a small and tidy person who seemed old to me, but was most likely about forty-five. She knew everyone who came into the library and was unfailingly polite and professional. Sometimes she would comment on the size of my book pile, always large, or suggest something I might like, or ask me in a whisper if I had enjoyed a book. When I left, she would stamp a due date beside my name on the cards and smile as she said, "Come back soon, Mary. I know you will."

I would walk out into the bright sunlight or the gray skies and rain with a bundle of riches in my arms that I could hardly wait to enjoy.

My first year in town I read every interesting book in the children's section. I was outraged at the treatment of horses as shown in *Black Beauty*, and I wanted a mustang like the one in *My Friend Flicka*. My favorite novels were *Little Women*, *A Tree Grows in Brooklyn*, and *Sara Crewe*, now called *A Little Princess*.

At that time, many children's books taught us to aspire toward heroism. I was enthralled by how people coped with adversity and grew up to be heroes. I read about Helen Keller, Abe Lincoln, Eleanor Roosevelt, Madame Curie, Dr. Tom Dooley, and Dr. Albert Schweitzer. I read *Up from Slavery* by Booker T. Washington and a biography of George Washington Carver, the first books that educated me about race. These books reinforced the teachings of my mother, aunts, and grandmother, which were that good people act on behalf of others and that the most satisfying work is devoting oneself to a great cause.

I was inspired by *Death Be Not Proud*, by John Gunther, about the death of his brave son who as a child developed cancer. Gunther also wrote many books with titles such as *Inside Africa* or *Inside Europe*. He wanted Americans to understand the world from the point of view of faraway peoples. I loved his guides. I also read *A Child's Geography of the World*, *A Child's History of Art*, and *A Child's History of the World*.

My aunt Margaret told me that many people only know their friends and neighbors, but that readers are able to experience the lives of thousands of people from all times and places. I craved that experience—knowing how other people felt, thought, and behaved.

Reading lit a path into my future. I was constructing an identity beyond the bounds of family. And I was beginning to understand how big, complicated, and amazing the world truly was.

Around this time, I began playing what I called the globe game. I would spin our globe with my eyes closed and put my finger on it somewhere before I opened them. Then I would imagine myself in whatever spot my finger had landed. I tried to see the trees, sky, birds, and water. I imagined the children's clothing and toys, and the foods. I listened for the tinkle of bells or the calls of grown-ups at work. I yearned to visit every part of the world when I grew up.

With the librarian's guidance, I eventually read novels by Mark Twain and Charles Dickens and a great many others, including *Pride and Prejudice*, *War and Peace*, and *Les Misérables*. These books helped me inhabit worlds very different from my own and increased my sense of the wide range of human experiences. I came to understand that many people suffered as children. I was not alone, but part of a community of sufferers that included much of the human race. That realization was oddly comforting.

Over time, the library became my church and reading became my way of understanding the world. I built myself from books.

Reading offered me hope, soothed me in difficult moments, and gave me a sense of the immense complexity of the human spirit. There are all kinds of light in the world—from the sky, during moments of bliss and awe, and from the lemony circles on the tables of the Beaver City library.

House Calls

My mother was a sturdy woman with dyed auburn hair, broad shoulders, and long strong legs. People often asked if she was Frank Sinatra's sister; she resembled him all her life. She didn't have an expressive face, but I could read her eyes and notice the tightness around her mouth and jaws.

She dressed in high heels, a silk blouse, and a long, fitted skirt. Over this elegant outfit, she wore her white medical jacket. She always had a stethoscope dangling from her neck and carried a black doctor's bag that contained digitalis, morphine, aspirin, a blood pressure cuff, scissors, bandages, a thermometer, and a tourniquet.

Mother did everything required of a doctor in Furnas County. She conducted the school physicals and vaccinations, and she attended all the stock car races and home football games. On a weekly basis, she made rounds, at all the county's nursing homes, talking to staff and monitoring

every patient. At her office, she performed tonsillecto-
mies and hernia surgeries, set broken bones, delivered
babies, and suctioned rattlesnake bites. And the law
required her to conduct autopsies on all deaths in our
county. She was the coroner who accompanied the sheriff
to suicides and car accidents. No matter what happened
medically in our county, it was my mother's job to deal
with it.

We children often went whole nights and days without
seeing her. She might come in late and sleep a few hours
and be gone again before we woke up. She laughed about
the fact that old farmers would call her at 4:30 in the
morning to say, "Doctor, I've been suffering all night, but
I waited until morning to call so I wouldn't wake you."

Even when she was home, she had a small office off
our living room, and, if necessary, patients would stop in
after hours. That space was effectively the town's urgent
care and emergency room. She felt it her duty to care for
all people in our county whether or not they could pay.
I was proud of my mother, but I was lonely.

I missed her terribly, but I didn't resent her. She had
no choice. She couldn't let an appendix rupture because
it was Thanksgiving or tell the sheriff she couldn't go with
him to a car accident because she was playing Scrabble
with her kids.

From fifth grade on, I worked in Mother's office,
sterilizing rubber gloves, needles, syringes, and when I
could, riding with her to the nearest hospitals. Almost

every day and sometimes twice a day, she made rounds. During the day, I would read in the car or in the hospital waiting room. I liked to go in and see the newborns lined up at the windows in the nurseries. At night, I would sleep in the car until Mother returned, then wake up for a conversation on the way home.

I would also accompany her on house calls to farms. Usually these occurred when an old person was dying and couldn't be moved. She would sit with the family until her patient passed. Back then, doctors couldn't do much but offer solace and that was all people expected. However, these calls could take hours.

One afternoon we pulled into the farmyard of a man who neglected his children. They were a sad-looking lot, skinny with pale faces and dull hair. This father wouldn't allow the kids to be vaccinated or play with other kids. My mother treated the family for free because, as she said glumly, "Otherwise, they would get no care at all."

But this day Mother had been called to the farm because the wife was having a miscarriage. When we arrived, we were surrounded by growling, slobbering dogs who looked like they wanted to kill us. The farmer came out, called the dogs off, and chained them to a pole. Only then was it safe for my mother to go inside.

"Don't get out of the car," she said. "Those dogs are strong enough to break those chains."

On the drive home she reflected on something the man had told her. He had said, "When I was a boy I wanted a dog but my dad wouldn't get me one. I hated him for that. I've made sure my kids could have dogs."

My mother noted that people's ideas of how to be a good parent varied widely and that parents often gave their children what they never had, not necessarily what the children wanted or needed. I thought about that conversation for several days. My parents thought they were good parents: we had food, clothes, toys, and anything we wanted to buy at the store to eat. They took us on trips and out for ice cream. Neither of them had these things as children. I was grateful for what they had given us, but I wanted more attention from my mother and more calmness from my father. I realized that no children get everything they want.

Sometimes at the farms there would be children I could play with. I loved playing in barns, the most delightful of all play spaces. Light would filter in through the windows and cracks, and just like the girl in Rumpelstiltskin, it would spin straw into gold. If I stayed alone in the car, I always had a book with me. At night I would sleep with a blanket and pillow that we kept in the back seat. I would wake up when Mother returned, and we would talk on the way home.

I liked driving through the country at night. The stars were bright and low, and the constellations were beautiful in their fixedness. Often, we would see something marvelous such as a cornfield alight with lightning bugs, a falling star, or the moon rising.

The farms were scattered across a wide area, with usually only a light over the barn and a few lights in the windows of the house. These lights were a comforting reminder that we were small on the great horizon of earth, but also that we were not alone.

During our rides to the hospital or on house calls, my mother told me story after story about her life as a girl on a ranch during the Dust Bowl years and the Great Depression. Her father had been the last man in the county to give up his horses for a tractor. Mother's first horse was a gray named Felix; her second was Blaze. She rode these horses to check on cattle. She always carried a long bullwhip with a foot of wire at the end. When the horse stopped quickly, she knew to look for a rattlesnake. Then she would kill it with her whip.

From her, I learned stories of disasters from throughout history, from Marie Antoinette and the Russian Revolution to the Hindenburg, the Donner Party, the Titanic, and the Lindbergh baby's kidnapping. She loved the concepts of fate and destiny. How do we handle the circumstances that befall us?

She was interested in how people behave when their backs are up against the wall. That is when character is elucidated.

Together we would unpack the moral choices people made on the Titanic's deck or in the Donner Party. One of her lessons was that we always have the choice to behave well, no matter the circumstance.

I loved these stories. They generated questions for me. I wondered if my character would be tested. Would I be brave and self-sacrificing? What was my destiny?

I also learned medical history from my mother. She had a way of making stories about scientists into moral lessons. For example, she told me about the Hungarian physician Ignaz Semmelweis. He had worked in a hospital where many women died in childbirth. One day he noticed that doctors left the room where they were doing autopsies and went right into the delivery room. He suggested that the doctors wash their hands before delivering babies. Sure enough, infant and mother mortality dropped, but Semmelweis was scorned when he talked about antiseptic procedures. Instead, he lost his job and was sent to prison. He was beaten by prison guards and died eight days later. It was another fifty years before physicians accepted his theories around hand-washing and cleanliness.

The moral of this story was that sometimes, even when you are right, no one will believe you, but if you know you are right, you need to speak the truth.

My mother also told me about titration. The example she gave was digitalis. A very small amount of digitalis can help people in heart distress, but even a slight amount more than necessary can kill them. She said that what we knew of titration could generalize to all of life, that happiness and success can be achieved by knowing the right proportions.

Mother also told me about her patients. I was educated early and firmly in confidentiality, and I never violated her trust. My mother had a way of telling stories so that they were full of both drama and lessons about the human race. At the end, she knotted her stories tight with profound and surprising points.

For example, she told me about an old man who came to her office after he had been sprayed with pesticide by a crop duster. He told the receptionist that he was having trouble breathing. She said my mother was very busy and he would have to wait his turn. Even though he was in great distress, he waited quietly. Finally, he keeled over almost dead from the poison on his body and in his clothes. About this man my mother said, "He was so polite, he would rather risk death than cut in line."

Once an old farmer brought his whole family in for their vaccinations, and he asked Mother to fill out an insurance form for him. My mom gave him a checkup and filled it out. A month later, after his life insurance application was accepted, he walked into the barn after dinner and shot himself in the head. After that, when men showed up for life insurance physicals, Mother asked them about their finances and depression.

Mom cared for a girl whose mother had gotten angry at her and scalded her head while washing her hair. There were no laws against child abuse until 1962, and in the 1950s, doctors had no way to deal with it. In fact, many people beat their children in those days. There was little my mother could do about the woman's actions. She told the daughter that if she was threatened or hurt again, she could come live with us.

Another girl did come to live with us. Bernice was a quiet, sad girl who did the dishes and played cards with us, but rarely participated in any of our family activities. I could tell by her sallow skin, wild eyes, and frightened demeanor that something bad had happened to her. At the time, my mother wasn't straightforward about why Bernice moved in with us, but, years later, she told me that Bernice had been sexually abused by her father. Bernice stayed with us for several months until she moved to live with her aunt from another town.

My mother died in 1992, but I still feel she's with me. She could be on a house call or at her office. Waiting for her comes naturally to me. When she was alive, she was often absent, and now that she's dead, she is often present. When she comes to me in my sleep, it doesn't feel like a dream, it feels like I have been sleeping in the back seat of the car. I hear the car door open and she says softly, "Mary, I'm back." She gets in the car, and we drive past the twinkling lights of the little farms. She tells me a story.

Storytelling

I was the oldest child in our neighborhood, and I organized games and projects for a roving band of kids aged six to twelve. I choreographed adventures in which we played orphans who must save ourselves, sailors on a ship in a hurricane, pioneer families, or students at a country school. I was always the teacher, and I liked to conduct spelling bees and geography quizzes.

We spent a whole summer acting in a story based on Ian Serraillier's book *The Silver Sword*. In this book, three enterprising children were abandoned in Warsaw after their parents were kidnapped by the Nazis and sent to factories to work. The daughter started a school for her brothers and for homeless children in the city.

In our play, the root cellar was our bombed-out building. I was the teacher, and my brothers and the neighborhood kids were my students. While I "cooked" or prepared lessons, the others foraged for food or wood.

Jake proudly brought in some green apples from a nearby tree. John found firewood and an orange crate we used as a table. We were enterprising children, and day after day, we survived the dangerous Nazis, the landmines, the rats, and the cold and hunger. We took pride in being able to care for one another in a disaster.

When I played alone, I often just walked country roads pounding a stick and making up happy stories in my head. Or, hanging up clothes, I would invent stories about sock couples or towels and washcloths (mothers and children). Doing dishes, I would create stories around the crockery and silverware. I really couldn't stop myself from creating these imaginary worlds.

Just like my parents, I liked to stay busy. I spent the morning in my mud pie bakery. I insisted Mother leave me with a large order such as three chocolate pies, two dozen oatmeal cookies, a dozen cupcakes, and two loaves of bread. Under the elm tree in the dappled light, I would work at the Bluebird Bakery made of boards and old cookware. I would mix my ingredients—gravel, dirt, small rocks, leaves, and sand—according to the recipe and then "bake" the results on flat boards in the sun. I would picture in my mind the parties and fancy dinners where my baked goods would be enjoyed.

Almost every night in the summer, my brothers and the neighborhood kids would gather at our house to lie in the grass, look at the stars, and hear my stories. Sometimes, Jake's best friend, Rex, showed up and so did Wayne and Leona, children of the woman who ironed our clothes. Jeanie was there and also Mike and Spike, twins whose dad was in prison. They lived with their grandparents and rarely mentioned their parents, although Spike told us that his dad knew Charles Starkweather, Nebraska's first serial killer.

The girl who lived behind us also came. Lana was not very imaginative, but she liked any games we created. She was flat-footed and chewed on her hair constantly. When her parents rang their cowbell, she immediately took off for home. Lana was in constant trouble at school and her family didn't go to church, scandalous behavior in our little town.

Because we were on the edge of town, we had clear views of the western and northern skies. The sky was blacker then and the stars more numerous. The Milky Way was so filled with light that it really did resemble a path made of milk. These stars were layered and looked both closer and farther away than stars do now. We kept count of shooting stars. Whenever I saw one, a reso- nating light fell through my heart.

One particularly beautiful August night, Jake noticed green lights in the northern sky. We all ran out to the gravel road that curved around our lawn and peered at the lights. Mike suggested it was a flying saucer and Lana thought we might be witnessing an atom bomb.

As we watched, a green plume billowed almost to the crown of the sky, then faded, then flashed again. Next, pink explosions danced on top of the green, and then flashes of blue and purple shot up into the Milky Way.

We stopped talking except for exclamations of joy. Then, as the kaleidoscope of light danced and swirled, Jeanie began dancing along with the lights. Soon we were all dancing and whooping, looking north, overtaken by the magic of this experience.

The light show went on and on. My mother came out to watch, and she explained that we were seeing the northern lights made by solar winds that changed the ions in our atmosphere. By then we had worn ourselves out with dancing. We flopped back on the grass as the giant plumes, created with better-than-Disney colors, rose and fell. I was washed in the same sense of wonder that I felt watching the KOA fountain lights.

The northern lights were the miracles of that time and place. I saw them as a gift from somewhere faraway, yet magical. It was as if light had somehow been transmuted into colored music. That night I assumed I would see those lights again and again. I had no idea how rare these dancing clouds of light would be in my life. I had not yet been schooled in impermanence.

I loved making up stories about the neighborhood kids. I would tell a story about Jake and Rex racing into a burning hospital to save the patients. Mike and Spike would become famous baseball stars and live in mansions filled with friends. Wayne and Leona would go on a trip around the world and have many adventures. Jeanie would become a heroic nurse who created a cure for cancer. And Lana, the homeliest of our lot, would become Miss America. I created these stories on impulse and because they made the children happy. I wanted them to have more faith in themselves and to see more bright possibilities in their futures.

As children, we greatly benefit from nurturing and empowering stories. We are fortunate if we have people who tell us these stories. As adults, we need to be able to tell these stories to ourselves.

Girl Scout Cookies

Time passed much more slowly when I was a girl, not only in my own life, but also in the life of our town. Stores opened at eight and closed at five. There were blue laws that kept all business shut on Sundays. A whistle called people to breakfast at seven A.M., home for lunch at noon, and again home at six P.M. in time for dinner. For everyone but the farmers, summers were especially lazy. No one had air-conditioning or television, so after dinner, most adults sat on their front porches and visited with neighbors.

The school year ended with Memorial Day and started again after Labor Day. We had no summer camps and few extracurricular activities. Some boys played baseball, but my brothers didn't. A few girls took piano lessons or belonged to Future Homemakers of America, but I kept busy working at my mother's office and reading. And we all spent time at the swimming pool under the buttery light of the Nebraska sun.

When I was eleven, I joined the Girl Scouts. I was an indifferent scout. I hated crafts, sewing, and decorating and was only interested in the nature badges, earned by building campfires, camping, and identifying birds. However, I loved selling cookies.

The first cookie season, I decided I was going to be the champion salesgirl in our town. Every afternoon I would put on my forest green uniform, a white blouse, my sash with its badges, and a yellow scarf and bike around town in the bright sun, stopping at every house that didn't have another Girl Scout in it to pitch Thin Mints and Peanut Butter Patties to whoever would listen.

Traveling around on my own and seeing how people lived was a great educational experience. Many older people were lonely and would invite me in. One elderly woman told me, "Everyone I love is in the ground now."

I visited with people who were grateful to talk for as long as they wanted. I learned how to ask questions and to listen. I found it was good to ask about weddings and mothers, but it could be risky to ask about fathers. Many people had sad or angry memories of distant or abusive fathers.

I loved their stories and lessons about how adults feel and behave. A bowlegged old man had been a rodeo rider, and he showed me pictures of himself as a young man on his horse, Jupiter. He said, "I broke ten bones at the rodeo and I don't regret a thing. I'd still do it if I could."

One older man named Mr. Graber greeted me on the porch of his small house and talked for a long time about his rheumatism and his dog. He was rarely able to leave home, and he said I was his first visitor of the week. His only other regular visitor was the grocery delivery boy. Mr. Graber had a small brown pug named Bullet who jumped into the old man's lap when he sat in his rocker. Mr. Graber said Bullet couldn't do tricks, but he could understand thoughts. "I don't even have to say it," he said. "I just think it and Bullet knows what I mean."

I patted Bullet and expressed sympathy for Mr. Graber's health problems. I told him I admired his strength. At the end of our talk, I had almost forgotten about the cookies, but he bought ten boxes. I visited him once a month until we moved away.

Down the street from Mr. Graber, I stopped at a house with five sons, two of whom were on the high school football team. The father ran our city's locker where most families stored meat. He worked long hours and came home too tired to be of much help to his wife. The weary-looking wife bought ten boxes. I hoped this would save her some baking.

A classmate from school answered the door of a small white house. I liked Francis, but I never saw her except at church. When I knocked on her door, she invited me into the living room where her father lay on a daybed. He had suffered a work injury years earlier and could only lie or sit in his bed. Mr. Baker asked Francis to bring us each a bowl of ice cream.

She and I sat by his bed, and we talked and laughed. He praised Francis for the care she gave him. He said, "She's only eleven but she does all the cooking and cleaning. She irons her own clothes and cuts my hair."

When Francis walked me out, she told me, "I am lucky to have such a good dad. He is never too busy to listen."

At the end of the season, I stood proudly at an award ceremony as our troop leader, my mom's nurse, presented me with a Number One certificate and a bouquet of peppermint-striped carnations. My mother came to that ceremony, which was the best part, since she so rarely was able to come to my events. Of course, I liked receiving an award, but the true satisfaction for me was in the process, not the results. Selling these cookies met three needs of mine. I was out in the afternoon sunlight every day, I was working, and I was talking to people. I wished we had a cookie sale all year long.

III

In Another Light

Shelling Peas

My mother's parents lived in Flagler, Colorado, a railroad town that was part of a line of similar towns built seven miles apart from Kansas City to Denver. Seven miles is how long a steam train could go without needing to restock on coal and water.

My grandfather had ridden a horse to the area, built a sod house, and "proved up" the land. A year later my grandmother joined him on the ranch, which was one hundred acres of sand and sagebrush that had briefly greened in the early part of the century, only to go dry in the 1930s.

Neighbors helped them build a two-story house, a big barn, a smokehouse, an ice cave, and a root cellar. Grandfather planted wheat and ran cattle. Grandmother planted a big garden, milked the cows, raised the chickens, cleaned, cooked, and washed clothes. Even though both my grandparents had graduated from Peru State Teacher's

College in 1907, they spent their working lives on this land, barely scratching out a living for themselves and their five children.

By the time I was a child, my grandparents had sold the ranch and moved to a small stucco house on a corner lot in town. Grandfather planted peach trees and built a cement wood-fired grill in the center of the yard. In the summer we feasted on hot dogs, beans, and homemade ice cream in the peach orchard.

It was a delicious experience. In eastern Colorado, the air cools at night and has a crispness to it, as if it had blown down from the mountains. The peach trees were filled with birds twittering away as they settled in for the evening. Wood smoke from my grandfather's grill curled into the treetops. The hot dogs sizzled as we roasted them on specially carved weenie sticks. Nearby, my mother cranked the ice cream freezer, and my grandmother carried out plates of sliced tomatoes and cucumbers.

My grandfather was a useful man. In that era, many women didn't know how to drive, and Grandfather drove all my grandmother's widowed friends to church, the grocery store, and the doctor's office. He also helped these women understand their finances. That was another skill many women didn't have, since men generally managed the money.

Grandfather kept a few cattle on a ranch just outside town. He raised huge cabbages, then he used his kraut cutter to turn them into sauerkraut. He cared for the yard and orchard, picked the peaches, and buried meal leftovers in his garden for compost.

He and my grandmother canned all their food for winter, and I remember going with him down to the cellar. The walls were lined with jars filled with jewel-colored peaches, plums, beets, and pickles. Two shelves were reserved for jarred beef, and many more shelves were for homemade ketchup and tomato juice. In the corners of that cellar gunnysacks were filled with potatoes, turnips, and rutabagas. Onions hung on long lines from the ceiling. This cellar signaled plentitude.

Every afternoon grandfather walked downtown for the mail and a game of checkers at the pool hall. He had a gray leather case for his portable checkers set that he carried everywhere. When he visited relatives, he would find the pool hall and challenge the best players to a match.

He was a bald, sturdy old farmer in overalls and a felt hat. He had a large lump on the back of his neck that my mother called a wen. He adored his wife and frequently mentioned his good luck in marrying a schoolteacher. He was a whistler, a true sign of a happy man.

Yet all of his life he had an unusual habit. He would walk to the door and call into his house, "Anybody home?" If no one answered, he would find an outside chore until a family member returned.

My grandfather loved poetry and would recite favorite poems—"The Charge of the Light Brigade," "The Song of Hiawatha," and "Casey at the Bat." He also wrote poetry, in the style of Robert Service. I still own a copy of the modest collection my grandfather wrote and bound in heavy turquoise paper called *My Poems*. It includes poems with titles like "The Mother of My Babies" and "Our Country Club," named for the group of friends who shared meals and played cards on Saturday nights.

Grandfather liked to joke around. He would say, "I have a Roman nose, it roams all over my face." He entertained us children with magic tricks, limericks, and riddles. Every night after dinner, he would set up the card table, and we would play hearts or rummy, or later cribbage and pinochle. I loved him, and although he loved me too, I was just one of fifteen grandchildren to him.

My grandmother, though, always managed to make me feel as if I were her most important visitor. I was a skinny, unkempt girl with few social graces. And yet, in spite of a houseful of people for whom she had coffee to make and cooking to do, it was my grandmother who really saw me.

She wore rayon shirtwaists, thick hose, and boxy black shoes. Her wispy silver hair was pulled back in a knot and covered with a hairnet. She had clear blue eyes that sparkled when she smiled, but she was a dignified woman, known for her rectitude. Had she lived in a later era, I think my grandmother would have been a minister or a professor of English or philosophy. Instead, she spent her time doing the constant backbreaking work that farmwives did in the 1920s and 1930s.

When we arrived at her place, I usually headed right for her ceramic pig jar that was always filled with fresh gingersnaps. When I would say, "This is my favorite cookie," she would answer, "I know. That is why I made them."

My grandmother loved books as much as I did, and when I visited, she always had library books for me to read, plus the latest volume of Reader's Digest Condensed Books. She also subscribed to *Reader's Digest*, and in its pages, I learned about Lizzie Borden, Amelia Earhart's fateful journey, Sacco and Vanzetti, and Julius and Ethel Rosenberg. We would read side by side and then talk about what we had read. Like my mother, her discussions plumbed for moral lessons.

Grandmother held my hand and called me "My Mary." After every meal, she asked me to do dishes with her. Others helped us clear the table and then the two of us would stand in front of her double sink with its window facing south. She washed and I would rinse and dry. One of the first times this happened, I whispered, "Let's do these dishes slowly."

My grandmother smiled and agreed, knowing it meant I wanted plenty of time to talk. She asked me to tell her all about my friends and about the books I was reading. She listened approvingly and said, "Choose your friends as carefully as you choose your books."

The next time we did dishes, my grandmother asked me, "Shall we work slowly?"

Grandmother gave me my first nickname, "Bright Eyes." At the time, I thought it was because I could thread a needle for her when her old eyes could no longer see to do it—and because I was her official finder who looked for small items she had lost. Now, I think perhaps she intended a deeper meaning. She may have noticed I was curious, a watcher, a person who wanted to drink in all the information and experience I could. I think a Bright Eyes could spot another Bright Eyes.

My favorite activity with my grandmother involved what we called "cooking outside." Grandmother would put on her apron and carry out her simple tools, a white bowl and a battered old colander. We would pull two chairs under her ash tree and spend the afternoon destemming gooseberries or shelling peas. As we worked, I would talk to her about my life. She listened carefully and often told me something important such as "We are put here for a purpose. Our job is to leave the world a better place than we found it." Or, "It is better to have one true friend than to be popular."

Sitting outside on hot summer afternoons, I loved to look at my grandmother with her radiant face filled with love and intelligence. Above us the sage-colored leaves of the ash tree rustled in the ever-present wind. The light was dappled and dancing, and it filigreed the edges of each leaf with silver. This light was sprinkled on our clothes and arms as if we were a blessed part of it. It embraced us and took us in.

I am not sure I have ever been happier than during those moments of dappled light under the ash tree. Grandmother sensed how much I needed attention and she gave it to me. She understood the goodness in me, and through her eyes, I began to see myself. Her understanding helped something green and true inside of me grow. Grandmother was one of the first people who did the hard work of loving me into existence.

The Coffin and the Chenille Bedspread

Our family visited Mother's parents about once a month. Their house had two small bedrooms, a combination living and dining room, a mudroom, and a kitchen with a bathroom right beside it. Because Flagler was a quiet town of only a few hundred people, most of them friends of my grandparents, there were no locks on their doors.

When Grandfather was mucky from working in the garden or with cattle, he would leave his shoes and overalls in the mudroom, walk through the kitchen, and take a bath while conversing with my grandmother as she cooked dinner a few feet away.

When we visited, my parents slept in the guest bedroom with my sister, Toni. I slept on the couch, and my brothers slept beside me on the floor. I liked the closeness to my family, and especially to my grand-mother, who slept about thirty feet away.

One day my grandfather had an idea for a new sleeping arrangement. A neighbor had purchased a refrigerator and given my grandfather the large wooden box it was shipped in. He removed the long rectangular lid and cleaned up the container. He smoothed and varnished the wood, and decided that, with a foam pad placed at the bottom to serve as a mattress, the inside of the box would be my bed.

When we arrived one summer morning, he proudly showed me his creation. My grandmother had already put bedding inside. It had been placed against the wall in my parents' bedroom, my least favorite room in the house. Its only window was small and faced north. The walls were dark green and the heavy furniture was the color of burnt umber crayons.

As I stood staring down into this "bed," my grandfather examined my face for a happy reaction. I felt a tight ball of flame form in my chest, and I had trouble breathing. I wanted to be polite and didn't want to hurt his feelings, but I knew I could not handle this coffin. I was terrified. I blurted out, "I can't sleep in that."

My grandfather left the room quickly without looking at me. I stood there struggling with two emotions at once. I knew I had been a bad girl, just like the time I bit the doctor, and I was frightened my mother would make me sleep in the box.

Sure enough, my mother came into the dark room. We sat down on the bed and she said, "Mary, you need to sleep in the new bed. Your grandfather is so proud of it."

I shook my head and said, "I won't do it."

My mother's jaw tightened and her eyes narrowed. She looked at me and said, "Be a good girl now. This isn't like you."

I explained to her that I couldn't force myself into a small coffin-like space. I didn't know the word *claustrophobia*, but I told her I would die if she made me sleep in that box.

I didn't expect my words would move her and they didn't. She had no tolerance for what she called neurosis. She dealt with people every day who were in physical pain, dying, or facing genuinely frightening situations. "Mental cases" were not worthy of her attention.

She said, "I want you to get in that bed now. Try it out and you'll see it is fine."

I had no choice. We didn't disobey our parents. I thought quickly about how I could survive doing what my mother asked. Finally, I turned away from her, shut my eyes, and stepped into the box. I hoped that if I didn't see where I was, I could manage.

However, I knew exactly where I was. Even worse, I imagined myself underground with someone shutting the lid on me. I could almost hear the sound of dirt hitting the coffin's lid. My chest hurt and I couldn't breathe. I leapt out of that box like it was on fire.

"I'll run away from home if you make me do this."

I looked at my mother, who seemed as mixed up as me. She didn't want to hurt my grandfather either. She was a good girl too. But, in spite of her disdain for mental cases, she believed me at last.

She said, "Go lie on your grandparents' bed for an hour and think about your behavior."

My mother had no idea how relieved I was. I didn't mind thinking about what had just happened. I wanted to understand it myself. She also didn't realize how much I liked my grandparents' bedroom. It was no bigger than the guest bedroom, but it had two windows and was filled with light from the east and south.

The white chenille bedspread was luminous in the morning sunshine. I lay down and rubbed my cheeks against its nubby blessedness. I felt the warmth of the eastern sun and breathed in the fresh air that smelled of peaches. Suddenly, I felt engulfed in bliss. The light, the bedspread, the breeze gently blowing the diaphanous white curtains—it was all holy to me. My relaxed body filled with warm white light.

I don't know how long I remained in this exalted state. I remember I tried not to move because I didn't want it to disappear.

At some point, my mother came in and broke the spell. She said, "It's lunchtime. Jake is going to sleep in the new bed. You owe your grandfather an apology."

I stood up and shook myself off. I was waking from a trance, yet remnants of bliss flittered inside me. I floated to the kitchen and told my grandfather I was sorry. He cleared his throat and looked away, but he said, "It's all right. I don't want you to be unhappy."

I truly was sorry; I didn't want to hurt anyone's feelings. Yet I also was proud. Usually my only thoughts were about pleasing others, doing the right thing and not upsetting people. For once, I had stood up for myself.

Jake passed me the coleslaw. My grandmother handed me a glass of buttermilk, and slowly I returned to the world of ordinary human interaction. I looked into the faces of everyone around the table and felt grateful to be included. My thoughts shifted ahead to a long afternoon of playing in the peach orchard and cooking with my grandmother.

Harbor Lights

As Christmas approached, Dad announced, "Your mother needs a rest, we're taking a trip to Padre Island."

A few days later we climbed into our big Oldsmobile and headed south. Dad said, "It's over a thousand miles, but we'll be there tomorrow."

In those days, there were no interstates, so instead we drove through one small town after another from Beaver City, Nebraska, all the way to Port Isabel, Texas.

Heavy snow was falling on the Christmas lights of the little towns in Kansas and Oklahoma. Wreaths hung from wires across main streets, and brightly decorated trees sparkled in the windows of grocery and hardware stores. Nativity scenes blanketed with snow adorned the lawns in front of the churches.

In Coffeeville, Kansas, Dad noticed a sign in a café window that read, "20 hamburgers for a dollar." He pulled over, walked in, and soon returned with a greasy bag full of burgers. He took a couple, handed our mom a couple, and threw the rest back to us children. We devoured them like we were piranhas in the Amazon.

Texas had no speed limits, and, when I woke in the night, the speedometer was showing 110 mph. Dad was smoking and listening to country music on the radio. His window was open, and I could smell dust and mesquite in the air. We had left the cold far behind.

I lay on the narrow shelf between the back seat and the rear window. From my berth, I could see the stars and the road receding across a vast, unfenced landscape. Rocking with the motion of the car and imagining the ocean, I fell back to sleep.

By early afternoon the next day, we were on the Gulf Coast in a bungalow right by the ocean. This was our first beach vacation, and we siblings were giddy with excitement. Beside our bunk beds, we opened our small suitcases and pulled out our swimsuits.

At water's edge, everything felt amazing—the glow of the Texas sun in December, the warm, soft sand under my feet, and the briny smell of the air. My brothers, Toni, and I ran into the water and splashed around in its salty waves. Jake and John were long-limbed, bony boys with flat-top haircuts. I can still see them falling into the cresting waves simply for the joy of it. Toni was much younger, but she plunged bravely into the water as well. It wasn't long before we figured out how to body surf, and we devoted the rest of our trip to that immense pleasure. We were exploding with energy and as wild as weasels.

One glorious day folded into the next. Except for frequent trips to the cabin for potato chips and cookies, we were outdoors from sunrise until sunset. My mother took long naps, swam laps far from shore, and played with us in the waves. A hundred yards down the beach, our father fished, catching mostly sharks, but also mackerel, drum, and sea trout. Whatever he caught, he cleaned and fried for dinner. He served up big platters of steaming fish that, no matter how many, we famished children could always finish.

A couple of afternoons, he bought pounds of fresh shrimp to boil. Our parents ate the whole shrimp—head and shell included. We children pulled off the heads but ate everything else. To this day, I enjoy the crunchiness of the shrimp shells and tails.

One night after dinner, Dad packed up to go fishing on a pier a mile away. I asked if I could come along, and, surprisingly, he agreed.

He stopped to buy bait and beer, and he bought me an orange soda. I held the cool glass bottle with such gratitude. On the pier, Dad set up his fishing station, opened a beer, and lit a cigarette.

He didn't talk much, but when he hooked something, I would watch him pull it in. That night he was catching flounder. Those silvery fish, trimmed with yellow and mother of pearl, were the prettiest fish I had ever seen. When my father held up his catch for me, it felt as if he were showing me the moon.

I stood a few feet away from him, just taking in the splashing sounds of the water hitting the pilings underneath us and the shushing sounds of the waves breaking on shore. The air smelled like fish and seaweed with a hint of gasoline. The stars hung low and liquid in the moonless sky.

Far beyond the shore, shrimp boats rocked with the waves, their red and white lights bobbing. Closer to shore, smaller boats, some with blue lights, swayed gently. Lights from the small hotels and houses flashed their reflections onto the dark waves.

Watching those lights catapulted me into another epiphany. All was right with the world. There was nothing to strive for, nothing that needed to be changed. I was aware of my dad humming a Glenn Miller song as he fished, my nubby orange-striped shirt, the lights, the smells, and the liquid air. I breathed it all in.

I willed myself to remember everything and to cache it deep in my memory. I never wanted the slightest detail to disappear. That night I taught myself the skill of storing moments of revelation and joy. It is a useful skill in a world filled with at least as much shadow as sunlight.

Prairie Dog Villages

S how me a village and I'll show you the world," Tolstoy wrote. Beaver City was my world, and I was old enough to navigate it on my own. I had a best friend, a pack of neighborhood kids, access to the small downtown and to mother's clinic. I could have my pick of adults and children to enjoy.

Alvin Rogers was our school's janitor and the bounty hunter who sold us coyotes. Spike and Mike visited their father in the state penitentiary once a month. Rex was the banker's son, although the only evidence of wealth in the family was a window air-conditioner. His mother had asthma, and his dad could afford this luxury.

Not all diversity was tolerated. Racism and anti-Semitism were rampant. Native Americans were a target of vitriol. People of color would have had trouble in our town, not from everyone, but from some. Homosexuals were also viewed as outsiders. The crippled son of the local pharmacist was gay. He once made the terrible mistake of trying to kiss a boy in his class. After that, he was teased mercilessly for the rest of his school years.

With limited news of the world, our universe was one another. Children played and attended school and Sunday school. Adults had church, supper clubs, reunions, and coffees. Conversation was an art form. Good storytellers and joke tellers were highly prized.

My friends and I had freedom. In the summer, we left our home in the morning and returned only for meals. We biked wherever we wanted to go. This wasn't always so easy. Large packs of roaming dogs sometimes followed us barking aggressively and nipping at our feet. Around such dogs, we lifted our feet onto the handlebars.

One hot July afternoon, Jeanie and I formed a girl posse and biked to the next town to see what kind of Popsicles were in their grocery store. We weren't good planners, and, on the hot asphalt with no water supply, we quickly lost our enthusiasm, but we pedaled on. In Arapahoe, we found a water fountain and rehydrated, then went inside to sample Popsicles. On the way home, with the sun even hotter and too tired to proceed, we stopped a few miles short of town. A man came along with an empty truck bed and carried us in.

Sometimes after dinner, my parents drove us to visit the prairie dog village. This was an enormous sandy area several blocks long and almost as wide. It was dotted with burrows that formed an underground city with food storage units, nurseries, and workstations. The prairie dogs were continually repairing their tunnels. On the surface, we could see hundreds of furry little dogs, standing on their hind legs chattering, chasing each other around, or scouting for snakes and black-footed ferrets. Rattlesnakes and red-tailed hawks dwelled all around and feasted on them daily.

My brothers, Toni, and I would sit on the hood and watch the ongoing spectacle of prairie dogs at work and play. The sky was enormous in that place and time. As the sun turned from lemon to gold to orange to red, the shadows lengthened on the entrances to the burrows. By the time the sun touched the horizon, all the dogs would be in bed.

We often stayed after the sun went down. The after-glow of sunset was the best part, the pink and apricot clouds, the light just touching the tops of the soft blue hills, the coolness exhaling from the earth and the first stars blinking on.

Our natural ecosystem was still rich, and we took it for granted that we would always have a healthy, sustain-able planet. The land around us was filled with birds, insects, and mammals. It was easy to catch all kinds of fish in the creeks and ponds. In the spring we caught tadpoles in the ditches.

In those days before factory farming and industrial agriculture, I didn't know the fresh clean place I lived in would turn into a county of hog farms that pollute the water and stink up the air. I thought the prairie dogs, and all the other beautiful animals, fish, insects, and birds, would be there forever. Now they have been almost entirely eradicated. I hope their populations are restored. I would like my great-grandchildren to be able to watch prairie dog villages at sunset.

Ozark Summers

Our summer vacations were always camping trips to the Ozarks. We set up our tent by Table Rock or Bull Shoals Lakes, and my father's family would come to visit. Dad was a different person when he was back where he had grown up, with the people he loved. Something in him seemed to wake up, and he acted younger and more comfortable in his own skin. He hardly ever slept down there, because he was too busy enjoying himself.

He never should have left Christian County, Missouri. His sisters and mother lived close together all of their lives, and the county was filled with cousins, aunts, and uncles. The Brays had migrated into the area in 1840 and have populated that place ever since.

During the Depression, poverty had forced Dad's family to separate. In the early 1930s when my father was twelve, his father had a psychotic break. He rode his horse to the state mental hospital in Sedalia and committed himself. He lived there the rest of his life. This mental illness left the family without a breadwinner and with a great deal of shame.

Dad's mother and sisters, Henrietta and Grace, moved into homes where they worked for room and board, and my dad lived in various sheds and caves along the river. While homeless, he attended high school and played basketball. Dad was popular, good-looking, and a great dancer, and, in spite of his hard circumstances, he had a good time during those years.

He bathed and swam in lakes and rivers and foraged for mushrooms and berries. He knew everyone in the area and people helped him when they could. When everyone was struggling to stay alive, there was no shame in being poor and homeless.

When the United States declared war on Japan and Germany, Dad enlisted to fight. After that, he spent most of his life far from his Ozark family.

On our visits to Dad's family, Mother relaxed in a way she could only do when we were far from our home. She loved camping, swimming, and waterskiing, and she was fond of most of Dad's family, but she wasn't enamored of the Ozarks. She thought the music was awful and the attitudes provincial.

She was a sophisticated woman who had lived in Los Angeles, San Francisco, and Honolulu. She had been a code cracker in the navy, and she had a master's degree in biochemistry. She liked opera and classical music. Weeklong vacations were fine, but she shuddered at the thought of living in the area.

My brothers and I loved Bull Shoals Lake, our big cabin tent, and the long days outside with our cousins, aunts, and uncles. The first few years, Grandma Glessie was there, but she died when I was nine.

Every day Aunt Grace and Uncle Otis would motor their houseboat over to our campsite. Otis was a dark-haired, slim man who sported a fedora with a feather in it, wore his slacks with a narrow white leather belt, and always had a pack of Camels in his shirt pocket. He made his money pumping gas or sitting on the porch of his general store selling insurance. Grace ran the store and post office inside. Otis didn't like physical labor, and all of his life, he figured out ways to use his intelligence and personality to avoid it. At barn raisings, Otis was the professional encourager who walked around congratu-lating other men on their work and asking if they needed water or any tools.

He met Grace when he was sixteen and teaching in her country school. In that place, at that time, anyone who made it through eighth grade could be a teacher. They eloped on Halloween. Grace wore a black silk dress to the wedding. When Otis and Grace moved into a tiny house with their three young children, they took in Dad and his younger sister Henrietta. It was so crowded that Dad slept on the floor under the kitchen table.

Otis took an almost paternal attitude toward my dad. He put up with practical jokes and ribbing from him. He just smiled his slow, lopsided grin and let it all slide by.

Apparently, Otis had been wild and hot-tempered when he was young, but by the time his children were grown and he was with our family, he had an easygoing, loving disposition. I never heard him raise his voice or swear.

Otis and Dad catfished on a small motorboat all night. They would come in at sunrise, clean fish, and make us breakfast of fried catfish and potatoes. They were close friends, but every now and then Otis would intervene to protect one of us kids. If Dad had been drinking and became angry, Otis would say, "Frank, these are good kids. Take it easy on them."

When she was young, Grace had been a dark-haired beauty, but by the time I knew her, her hands and face were worn from work. She struggled with depression, but found the natural world a great balm, foraging for pokeberries, watercress, and mushrooms. She knew the names of all wild creatures and plants.

Aunt Henrietta and Uncle Max would drive down to the lake most days. Uncle Max was built like a fire hydrant and very funny. He made his living selling, first for Dr. Pepper and later for a meat company. He was always the top salesman.

Max treated Aunt Henrietta like a queen. When he was present, she never opened a car door or pulled out a chair for herself. She fixed her hair and wore makeup. Her skin was soft as pillows. She sweet-talked everyone, calling us "Sugar," "Honey," and "Baby." She was a big talker, a joker, and a wonderful cook. She and Grace both showed up with delicious food—fried chicken, potato salad, thin-sliced cucumbers in sour cream, and chocolate cake.

My mother called our campsite "Snake Hollow." Our playmates were Max and Henrietta's sons. Steve was six years older than Paul and our official spotter in the water. This wasn't an easy job. If snakes surfaced, their heads looked just liked turtle heads and most of their bodies were underwater. Sometimes, they were invisible until they slid beside us. Even in the warmest water, I shivered when that happened.

Every now and then Steve shouted "Everybody out!" and we would all jump on the dock or head for shore until the snake slithered away. If it had a big, blocky head and a dark, thick body, it was a water moccasin. The lake was full of them and they could be aggressive. The shore had rattlesnakes and copperheads.

The Ozark summer air smelled green from all the wild plants and overgrown trees. Plants grew so quickly that I felt if I stood still, I would soon be engulfed with weeds and vines. The lake water was green and slimy from algae and as thick as soup.

We played in the water around a dock the size of a ping-pong table. When we were tired, we would climb out via a flimsy metal ladder and lie on the dock's slippery surface. Most of the time, this dock bobbed gently in the water, but when a speedboat went by, it rolled from side to side, and we had to hold on tight not to fall off.

We would lie on the dock for a long time, looking at the clouds, listening to the gentle slapping of water hitting wood, and munching on potato chips soggy from the general dampness.

As the afternoon wore on, the sun sparkled on the lake and the water turned iridescent as emeralds. The wooden dock glittered silver, and we children had all of life's riches—our tribe, the sun, the water, and our gently rocking, toast-warm dock.

The people from those long-ago green summers are still with me. They will always be with me because they made me. They are as much a part of me as my ribs or my vocabulary. I am mustard greens, turtle meat, and snake stories.

When I am gone, I will be a part of my grandchildren and yet-unborn great-grandchildren. My grandkids have been built by raspberries, nature walks, and my stories of heroic children. We all create each other.

Shafts of Light

Winters were colder and snowier in the 1950s than today, and it was a trial to walk up the steep hill to the school north of our house. Although girls could wear snow pants on the walk to school, we had to wear dresses in the building. The school itself was drafty, and many of us had chapped legs over the winter.

No one in my family listened to the radio for snow day announcements, and sometimes my brothers and I trudged all the way across town and up that hill only to realize that the building was locked.

In fourth grade I had an excellent teacher, a farmwife named Mrs. Oliver. She was a slender, dark-haired woman who had young children in the school. After the lunch recess, she allowed us to lay our heads on our desks while she read us adventure books. Her voice was crisp and clear, but gentle. Each chapter ended with a cliffhanger, and she dropped her voice for the dramatic last line.

Mrs. Oliver taught us to diagram sentences. When I went home at night, I did this for fun. In geography, we studied every country in the world, their capitals, their major rivers, and their main exports. Our tests required us to fill in maps of the continents with only the countries' boundaries demarcated. We drew little symbols for rice, cattle, cotton, and tungsten in the appropriate countries. I liked the precision and clarity of the work. Under Mrs. Oliver's tutelage, I felt as if we organized the English language and the entire world into something manageable.

Mrs. Oliver was the only teacher in Beaver City who could hold my interest. She conveyed her excitement about learning and intuited children's needs. She let me sit by a window and read when I wasn't busy. She allowed one restless boy to be her runner, and when he needed a break, she sent him all over the building on little errands.

Her classes were calm and orderly. There was a hum in the room that came from our collective engagement in the work of the day. The walls were filled with bright pictures of animals and flowers, and the shades were open so that we could see what was happening out-of-doors. My home life was disorganized and chaotic, and Mrs. Oliver's class allowed me to believe things could be otherwise.

Jeanie and I played hopscotch, jacks, and jump rope at recess. My brothers played marbles. I didn't like some of what I witnessed on the playground. I would see the sad children alone or hear kids teasing others about having germs. If they touched these "germy" children, they would run over to another child and rub the "germs" on him or her. The unfortunate victims of this constant teasing were already miserable enough. I was deeply troubled by all of this, but rarely had the courage to intervene.

My days at school felt operatic, with so much intensity and my yo-yoing emotions. Some days I had my feelings hurt or I felt bad about something I had done. When I walked out of school, I was often tired, hungry, and wound up.

Most afternoons I went to my mother's office to work. Alone in the back room, I calmed down as I washed and sterilized equipment or organized surgical packs. Then, during my sixth-grade year, an elderly woman came to my mother and offered to teach me how to make pottery and paint china.

After that, twice a week for the next two years, I walked to Mrs. Van Cleave's large white house on a corner lot. Mrs. Van Cleave was a Dutch immigrant who still had a slight accent. She was plump but compact, with soft, white skin and silver braids wrapped around the top of her head. She dressed in a housedress mostly covered by a white smock.

When I arrived, Mrs. Van Cleave would serve lemon bars and chamomile tea in hand-painted china cups. She would ask about my day, and within minutes I would be an unstoppable geyser of stories, reflections, and emotions.

After our tea, we would walk through the Van Cleaves' elegant, old-fashioned living room. A polished black piano was topped by a marble sculpture of a naked man, which Mr. Van Cleave had brought back from Italy after World War II. I would avert my eyes so I wouldn't see such a prurient figure. The room was rather dark, with curtains on the eastern wall. She explained this was necessary to protect her high-quality copies of Rembrandts, Cassatts, and Vermeers.

In contrast, the light in the pottery room was everything I could possibly desire. Late-afternoon sunshine poured in from the large, unshaded western windows. Golden dust motes from drying clay pots danced in the air, and shafts of light fell across the room and onto our worktable.

In this chapel of light, Mrs. Van Cleave and I sat side by side, rolling clay for pots, glazing recent creations, or edging a commemorative plate with gold leaf. As I chattered away, Mrs. Van Cleave occasionally nodded, but she rarely offered advice or opinions. Sometimes, she would say something quite simple but deeply comforting to me: "Tomorrow will be another day," or "We all make mistakes," or "You are a good student."

She kept track of my school projects and tests, and she knew the names of my friends. She inquired about my home life too, not in a prying way, but with true concern. She would ask if my mother had been busy or if my father was in town.

One story I told her was about my Dad and me. My father was raising pigeons in our backyard in hopes of selling them in fancy restaurants in big cities. He and I had been outside their cage, talking as we rinsed the water pans. I had told him I might become an English teacher. He turned off the water, looked carefully at me, and cautioned me to study to be a doctor. He said, "I'm afraid that with your figure and big nose, you will never marry. You need to be able to support yourself."

I had frowned and wrinkled my face in confusion. I had never considered the idea that I wasn't pretty. I looked just like most of my friends, slim, tanned, and healthy, and I had big blue eyes and long lashes. But that day I felt my nose and looked down at my flat chest and bony hips. I wished Dad hadn't told me I would never marry, but I believed him.

Mrs. Van Cleave looked stunned by my story. Finally, she spoke, "No doubt your father wants you to be secure financially. He has seen a lot of hunger and poverty. But he was wrong to say that. He is blind to your beauty, and, Mary, you are beautiful."

After she said that, I held her hand for a time before we returned to our clay pots.

During our lessons, I thought I was learning to paint and throw pots. In fact, I was much too clumsy and impatient to be a good artist. My pots turned out lopsided, my glazes uneven, and my gold leaf runny. Instead, during my time with Mrs. Van Cleave, I was receiving therapy. Years later, I learned from her grandniece that Mrs. Van Cleave had worried about me long before she approached my mother with her offer of free lessons. She knew I was a good girl who could use a little looking after, and she wanted to give me the gift of her attention.

Whenever I walked out of her study with its gorgeous late-afternoon light, I felt calm and cared for. My jangled mind had settled down. I could walk into my own house with something to offer my family, a listening ear, a peaceful heart.

There were two kinds of light in that studio—the shafts coming through the western windows in late afternoons and the love beaming from my teacher's heart. Just before we moved to Kansas, Mrs. Van Cleave gave me a large oil painting she had done of me. In it, I looked beautiful.

Heart Light

The women in my mother's family were hard-working, stoic, and resilient. Even though my grandmother didn't have the right to vote until after her third child was born, she rode her horse from farm to farm convincing neighbors to be vaccinated for smallpox. She spent her summers weeding, picking, and canning in a hot kitchen with a pump for well water. The family burned cow chips for fuel and went without coffee, tea, or sugar. Twice a week, on Saturdays for shopping and on Sundays for church, she rode to town in the family's horse-drawn wagon.

Yet somehow through all this rough work, my grandmother managed to maintain her status as a cultured lady. She valued education, books, and classical music and spoke softly and with dignity in all circumstances. Like Mrs. March in *Little Women*, she managed her anger and frustration internally and showed the world a kind, pleasant face. She neither complained nor exalted; rather, she appeared to live gracefully and with purpose in every moment.

My mother, Avis, was the third of four sisters, born in 1917. My three aunts were born in 1914, 1915, and 1918. Only Aunt Margaret was a stunning beauty. Avis was pretty, but both Betty and Agnes were rather plain, big-boned, sturdy women. During my childhood, they all lived in different states, but the sisters visited often and stayed long. These women were both self-sacrificing and opinionated, and they had an enormous influence on how I understood reality.

From the beginning, Betty was designated the one to work with my grandfather in the fields and barn. She took great pride in her ability to work as hard as any man. Just after high school, she married a man named Lloyd, who came through with a crew harvesting wheat. They homesteaded at the base of the Bitterroot Mountains near Sandpoint, Idaho, not far from the Canadian border, and raised five children there.

Betty became a teacher and later a school principal. She was strict but fair, with a deep love of children. Uncle Lloyd was a fireman, a logger, and a hunting guide. The sheriff called him for help when he needed to break up a bar fight or to have a bodyguard.

Lloyd had never been handsome, but in his forties, he had been kicked in the face by a horse. He refused medical treatment and wore a horseshoe-shaped scar from ear to ear and chin to hairline. He was a devout member of a fundamentalist church and made his children go to bed at seven P.M. He forbade television or rock and roll. When he discovered his kids listening to our 45 rpms, he gave them all a whipping with a willow switch. But then he churned us some strawberry ice cream.

Aunt Betty liked jokes, storytelling, cards, and outdoor games. She often invited me for a walk. On one of these walks, Betty let it slip that sex was lots of fun. I had never heard an adult say that. Her attitude toward sex was the same as it was toward everything else. "Follow the rules and enjoy everything that isn't explicitly forbidden."

Margaret, the second daughter, was the artistic one. She played both the piano and the violin. Because of her delicate build and sensitive personality, she was designated the "indoor daughter," assigned to help my grandmother. At sixteen, she was thrown from a horse and lay in the dirt for hours until her father came looking for her. Her badly broken arm became very infected. The townspeople took up a collection to send her to the Mayo Clinic.

When she arrived by train in Rochester, Minnesota, the horse cab driver who drove her to the clinic gallantly offered to visit her during her stay. After her surgery and two-week recovery, he proposed marriage. Margaret's elbow was permanently bent at a right angle. Her musical career was over. She married my charismatic Uncle Fred, and they moved to Whittier, a town in California.

Early on, Margaret spotted me as a curious girl who enjoyed art and literature. When we were together, we managed to take long walks or go for car rides. She considered my dad's conservative political ideas crazy and told me so. She also attacked his southern views on race.

Margaret drilled me about my reading and gave me suggestions. She liked Jane Austen, Willa Cather, Robert Frost, and John Steinbeck. She said, "Many people only experience one life, their own. But if you are a reader, you can experience thousands of lives from all times and places."

She told me that there was a big world of ideas that I was not exposed to in Beaver City. She told me about Emmett Till, the lynchings in the South, the Japanese internment camps, and Joe McCarthy. She taught me how to look at paintings and photographs. We talked about theater, and she encouraged me to never miss a classical music concert. How the two of us loved the word *culture*. No one can love that concept more than curious girls who grew up before television or the internet on farms or small towns far from the cities.

One summer when our family was visiting Whittier, Margaret and Fred hosted a fundraiser for Adlai Stevenson. My dad took my brothers to the beach to go fishing, but Mom and I stayed to help.

Margaret gave me the job of walking around their living room and onto their deck carrying large silver trays of sliced cheese, crackers, and olives. As I presented the tray to a thin, sad-looking man, I noticed he had faded blue numbers tattooed on his wrist. When I asked Margaret what that tattoo meant, she said he had been branded by the Nazis at Auschwitz.

I had heard about the Holocaust, but until I met this man, it seemed very abstract and far away. When I thought about him later, I felt my heart muscles contract.

One year Fred closed down his medical testing laboratory, and he and Margaret visited all of the Seven Wonders of the Ancient World. They were married almost sixty years, but she outlived him and married again. When she died of the flu in her early eighties, she was singing and dancing in a musical.

My Aunt Agnes, the youngest sister, married a man with an eighth-grade education. On their farm outside Flagler, Colorado, Agnes helped butcher cattle and pigs, cared for an apple orchard and a big garden, and managed an egg and cream business. She sewed most of the family's clothes and worked in the fields. The rest of the time she was cooking, cleaning, and caring for the couple's three children.

Uncle Clair was a tall, broad German with jet-black hair and the biggest feet I've ever seen. He was an auctioneer, and he bellowed even when he said grace. Like my father, he was conservative. He was easily agitated, and our family listened to many arguments between him and my equally opinionated Aunt Margaret. My dad would chime in occasionally, but Clair advanced such inane arguments that even my dad was hesitant to agree with him.

One evening, during a discussion of religion, I said I wasn't sure God existed. Clair responded, "You need to believe in Him because that way, if he exists, you'll be sure to get into heaven. And you definitely won't end up in hell."

I wondered to myself, "What kind of God would reward you for such self-serving behavior? And how does one manufacture belief?"

As a child, I wasn't fond of Clair. He would tickle us children even though we begged him to stop. He yelled at Agnes and ordered her about as if she were his servant. He didn't even call her by her name but instead referred to her as "woman."

Especially if she dared talk about books, he mimicked her cruelly.

Of all my aunts, I saw Agnes the most. She lived near my grandparents, and I often helped her pick fruits and vegetables or cook and do dishes. I stayed with her family when the wheat harvest crews came through. In her steamy kitchen, we would cook them two big meals a day. We would serve these meals in the dining room on a round table. At noon, we would carry sandwiches and lemonade to the wheat fields. Agnes served fresh baked pies at every meal. Pie was a staple in those days, like bread and butter.

Agnes dressed in simple shirtwaists and sturdy shoes. She didn't wear makeup or have her hair done. Any extra money went to the children, in particular to Zetah, her dark-haired daughter who always had pretty dresses and patent leather shoes. The one luxury item the family owned was a piano, and somehow, with egg money, Agnes scraped together enough to pay for lessons for Zetah.

Agnes and I could talk the legs off a chair, and we covered everything from the local news to family dynamics to the books we were reading. The light she gave me was the one she had to give, a simple love of who I was and a clear declaration of enjoyment when we could be together.

As he aged, Uncle Clair softened. He was still a bellowing clodhopper, but he was kind to me. He knew I liked homemade tomato juice, and he always had a jar ready to serve. When Agnes was in her eighties and ill with Ménière's disease, Clair made her milkshakes and fetched her blankets and books. It was sweet to watch her basking in Clair's loving attention.

I grew up observing all the different ways adults related to each other and raised their children. I loved the stories I heard in a family of storytellers. I heard the arguments and the ways they were resolved, and I acquired an early education in point of view.

I built special relationships with all the women in my mother's family. I sought them out and savored their conversations and affection. I imbibed their moral lessons—work hard, be loyal to family, and make the world a better place. No matter what was happening in my home life, I knew my grandmother and my aunts loved me.

By loving and nurturing me, my aunts taught me to care for myself and other people. They also helped me understand that I was worth something and had special qualities possessed by no one else. None of my aunts flattered me or offered fulsome praise. Rather, they listened to me, talked to me about their lives, and encouraged me to think big about my own life.

We are fortunate if we have extended family nearby to offer us these kinds of gifts. Light from the heart helps all of us build a self.

I V

Identity

The Burning Tree

In 1961, when I was twelve, my family moved to a town of eight thousand people in Kansas. My mother joined a clinic in the hope that it would cut down her workload.

When I started my freshman year of high school, I resolved to become a regular girl and participate fully in the life of my school. I played clarinet in the high school band, joined pep club, and even auditioned to be a flag twirler. I was not selected. However, I was class treasurer and a Snowball Queen candidate. In short, I succeeded briefly at being mainstream, but I wasn't really suited for it.

After two or three football games, I realized I didn't understand or care to understand football, and I didn't like uniforms or the pep club's cheers. I was intimidated by the cheerleaders, who reminded me of all the things I wasn't—athletic, sparkly, beautiful.

Some of the boys at the games teased me with crude sexual jokes. I blushed easily and made a good target. Mainly I was just bored and found myself wishing I were home reading or walking along the nearby creek.

Still, I had a wonderful assortment of friends. I walked to school with Maureen, a thin, rather morose girl who had an unpleasant father. When I visited their home, he never looked my way or spoke to me. Mostly, he sat in his armchair in the living room looking at his collection of pornography. I hadn't known such a thing existed. I was amazed Maureen's father would unapologetically examine such horrid pictures in his living room. Clearly, he didn't care about embarrassing his own daughter.

Maureen was a serious girl who read a great deal. We talked about books and schoolwork mostly, but sometimes about lofty philosophical ideas. We enjoyed these conversations so much that after school, we often walked each other back and forth to our homes a few times before saying goodbye.

Another friend of mine, Sue, was an excellent pianist whose mother taught piano. She had pale white skin and green eyes accentuated by her tortoiseshell glasses. Her father was quiet, like Maureen's dad, but not unfriendly. One day he shot himself. My mother told me that Sue was home alone when she walked down the basement stairs to do laundry. She found his body and his exploded head all over the storage room.

Because his death was a suicide, there was no funeral. People politely pretended nothing had happened. Sue skipped a week of school, and when she returned, neither I nor anyone else spoke of her father's death.

We had no ways to communicate about such dark events. In that time, most doctors didn't even tell people that they had terminal diseases. Instead they would say, "You need to go home and put your affairs in order." Cancer, like suicide, was a forbidden word.

Not all my friends came from sad homes, though. Nina was a doctor's daughter with endless pairs of matching skirts and cashmere sweaters. She was warm and extroverted, and was a cheerleader and homecoming queen. At the slightest opportunity, she and I would laugh ourselves silly.

These three girls and many others were part of a close group who had slumber parties, dances, and outings in the summer. We kept each other entertained.

Mr. Leon, my science teacher, while not charismatic, was hardworking, kind, and competent. He wore a tie of a different color every day of the week, and he kept a pen in his pocket that matched the tie. Under his tutelage I studied biology, anatomy, and physics. We did dissections in his class, but after our first dissection of a frog, I asked to be excused from this. I didn't want to study dead animals. It seemed to me there had to be a better way to go about understanding a frog or a pig.

I also refused to collect butterflies by catching them in a net and dropping them in a jar of chloroform. We were rewarded according to the number of species we identified and mounted on a foam board. I could not bear to kill a butterfly, and I sensed something deeply wrong in this way of studying nature. When Mr. Leon told me I couldn't be a scientist if I thought the way I did, I told him I didn't want to be a scientist.

When I left the school building, I would take deep breaths of the fresh air and look at the trees and sky with relief. I always left school needing a cooldown.

One day in particular is etched in my memory. It was in late October, and Maureen had stayed after school for a meeting. As I walked home alone, I drank in the deep blue sky. The trees were turning, and the world was gold, bronze, and scarlet. Leaves were skittering across the yards. Just near the hospital, before I turned south toward our house, I stopped in wonder at the sight of a crimson maple. It was a tree full of wind, its leaves shimmying in a manner that reminded me of a Van Gogh tree.

The afternoon sun enflamed the tree. I was stilled by amazement, not moving and barely breathing. Perhaps I was witnessing the Kansas version of the biblical burning bush. As I beheld this blazing maple, I learned a deeply spiritual lesson about how the world, uncluttered by a thought-stream, could dazzle and exhilarate. I was totally awake to the perfection of the universe and grounded in absolute reality, more beautiful and transparent than the world we call real. Over and over, I have found rescue in these burning tree moments.

Summer Solstice

During my high school years, my favorite place was a large sandpit about five miles from town. On summer afternoons, Nina, who was the first to get her driver's license, would take us to this sandy beach with clear water. Actually, there were two lakes connected by a narrow channel. The lakes were deep and grew colder as we swam farther below the surface. Allegedly, they were so old that fossils of prehistoric fish had been discovered by the dredging company that owned the pits.

Perhaps the owner was a local man with children, or perhaps it was just a less litigious time, but for whatever reason, we were welcome there free of charge and given the gift of being unsupervised by adults. We saw big machines and heard the sounds of earth-moving equipment, but no one ever approached us and asked us to leave.

Thanks to this generosity, we girls had use of a Yucatan-quality beach, surrounded by old cottonwoods.

We would arrive around lunch with our picnics in paper bags and thermoses of water or lemonade. After carefully selecting our spot for the afternoon, we would dine on chips and tuna fish sandwiches, or BLTs and cookies. Then, after the required hour of rest, we would run into the sparkling water.

The other girls just waded and splashed to cool down, but I swam laps across the lake and dived deep like a dolphin at play. Swimming in clear, cool water under a blue sky on an endless summer afternoon is one of life's best experiences. That water, with its temperature variations, currents, and soft textures, felt like a living being.

On shore, we lay on our big towels talking about boys, books, or our families. At that time one of the rites of puberty was learning to wear a girdle. One day Nina told us that a new supply had arrived at our local Bon Marché department store. She suggested we all buy girdles and wear them to the movies on Saturday night.

"I am not sure we need girdles," I said.

"Of course we do, we're teenagers now," Sue said.

Maureen chimed in, "Mary, we all need flat stomachs."

The next day I tried on a thick rubber tube that covered my body from waistline to thighs. I could barely pull it up and I wondered if it was too small. But the clerk told me that girdles were supposed to feel tight. That was the point, to hold me in. She said knowingly, "You've got to suffer to be beautiful."

Standing alone in the dressing room, I felt like a fool. I could barely breathe. A little roll of flesh squeezed out from the top of the girdle, which cut into my skin like wire. Within seconds, I made a decision that I've stayed with all my life. "I won't follow the fashions of the day if I don't like them. My motto will be comfort before beauty."

The next day at the sandpit, I told my friends my decision. They didn't want to criticize me, but Nina said, "You might not get a boyfriend if you think that way."

Another conversation was about our swimsuits. The other girls talked about styles and colors of swimsuits, where they bought swimsuits, and whether we should all buy bikinis. I asked my friends how they felt about their swimsuits. Later that day, I had a realization: I understood that I had almost no interest in objects or appearances. I only wanted to know about feelings.

Almost all of us were dating, and most girls were kissing and "making out," a quaint phrase that may not be used anymore. I wasn't kissing anyone, but I listened closely to my friends' conversations about these matters. I wanted to understand this mysterious process of being physically involved with a boy. What did it feel like to go steady, to go to second base or third base?

My friends clued me in on French kissing, wrestling matches in the back seats of cars, and lies boys told girls to trick them into "going all the way." I was intensely interested in kissing boys, but I was too afraid to chance it, doubting I could manage something that sounded so complex. I decided that I would wait until college to kiss a boy.

While I was the baby of the group on dating expertise, on books I was the mentor. I recommended Flaubert and Hemingway, Sinclair Lewis and Thomas Wolfe. At that time, most of the writers available at our library were men. But now, I wish I had read Virginia Woolf, Mari Sandoz, Jean Rhys, and Simone de Beauvoir.

In my senior year, I made the terrible mistake of reading Truman Capote's *In Cold Blood* about the murder of a Kansas farm family. That book terrified me and kept me awake for years with adrenaline-fueled insomnia. I remember telling my friends not to read it, that it was a kind of poison that none of us needed in our lives.

Because I wasn't interested in makeup, hairstyles, or clothing, I diverted the group to topics I did enjoy. I asked how their families worked: Did their parents fight? What were the family rules? How did they get along with their siblings? What were the dinner table discussions like?

Looking back, I realize that I was trying to see what normal looked like. My own family felt odd and out of place, and my parents were unusual in their habits. How did it feel to have a homemaker mother as all my friends did, and a dad who came home to quietly enjoy the evening?

By late afternoon we were sated with conversation. We lay on our towels and relaxed together. My friends enveloped me in the circle of caring I needed to have faith in my future.

The Light from Ideas

At the high school, we had two wonderful older teachers, Miss Meyer and Miss Fletcher, who lived together and shared a deep love of English literature. Both were heavy-bodied with eyeglasses and silver hair. They dressed in the manner of 1950s older women—shirtwaists, dark hose, and heavy black shoes.

They were strict, but inspirational in their passion for Shakespeare, poetry, and the great novels of the past. In their classes we read Chaucer, Poe, George Eliot, Thomas Hardy, and Austen. We also studied Blake, Whitman, Dickinson, and Elizabeth Barrett Browning. I liked all of these writers except Poe. I've always been too easily frightened to enjoy the spooky or macabre. Miss Fletcher brought her Sunday *New York Times* to school every week and gave it to me.

Except for the sports, fashion, and business sections, I read the *Times* cover to cover. I started with world news and the Book Review, but my favorite section was Arts & Leisure. As I learned about the plays, concerts, and gallery openings, I imagined that one day I would be part of this sophisticated culture.

In the *Times*, I found words to look up in *Webster's Dictionary*. I memorized their spelling and meaning and wrote down three sentences using them. I also worked my way through a book called *How to Build a Better Vocabulary*. Soon I knew all kinds of big words such as *uxorious, intransigent,* and *termagant* that I couldn't utilize in public. Still, I felt that someday I would be around people who knew these words, and I wanted to be ready.

I decided to form a Great Books Society at my high school where students could gather and discuss some of the world's most significant ideas. The librarian helped me announce and promote my meeting. When the time rolled around, I eagerly waited for my fellow students to arrive. Sadly, no one came.

My face felt hot and I was too embarrassed to look at the librarian. Eventually she came to tell me the school was about to close for the day. She said gently, "Many of the students are busy with other activities. I appreciate your effort."

Our town library was a stately Carnegie Library with a dozen wide steps up to heavy glass doors with brass handles. Inside this library, with its marble floors and high ceilings, were long wooden tables and rows of leather-bound books. This library was filled with light from windows high above us.

My freshman year, I read Charles Dickens, Mark Twain, Pearl S. Buck, James Michener, and Leon Uris. I devoured classic novels such as *Madame Bovary*, *The Magic Mountain*, and *Don Quixote*. For nonfiction, I read Rachel Carson's *Silent Spring*, Viktor Frankl's *Man's Search for Meaning*, and Bertrand Russell's *Why I Am Not a Christian*.

In Tolstoy's *The Two Pilgrims*, a man who traveled the world meeting people and spreading words of joy and love. I planned to do the same. I wanted to know every kind of person, every culture, and every point of view.

I read *Crime and Punishment*, *The Brothers Karamazov*, *War and Peace*, and much of Chekhov, Gogol, and Turgenev. I fell in love with *Anna Karenina* and have read it several times since. I was captivated by the "Russian soul." The tragedy and ecstasy of the Russians matched my own emotional range. They were people who suffered deeply and constantly. Life was always hard and often brutal. But they also could be swept away by great passions and moments of bliss.

The books I loved most considered the largest of questions: How do we lead a good life in all circumstances? Is there a God? If not, how do we find meaning in our lives? Why do we have wars? Why is good fortune distributed so unequally? These lit up my mind and gave me something besides my own life to ponder.

The first two years after we moved to Kansas, Dad lived with us. He tried to make a living selling life insurance, but he hated it. His misery seeped into the walls of the house. He was drinking heavily every night.

During the day he tried to be a good dad. He bought us kids go-carts, rock polishers, metal detectors, and a ping-pong table. He also purchased a speedboat and spent long summer days pulling us on water skis. We each had a tropical fish tank. For mine, I chose angelfish and tetras. Jake's tank had guppies with long tails, and John had red swordtails. Sometimes we mixed species with sad results. I learned never to name a cichlid after anyone I knew because they often turned out to be assassins.

Neither of my parents had the gift of empathy. Jake had the most trouble with Dad. He was an extremely gifted boy, painfully shy, and physically awkward. He was failing his classes, yet he read for hours a day and spoke in quotations and stories.

Our father thought he should be making A's and bludgeoned him about his failure to be a good student. Jake didn't argue with our father, but he couldn't obey him either. Over the years, our father never broke Jake's will, but he temporarily broke Jake.

I would come home from school to find Jake grounded in the basement. I would go down to visit him with some snacks and beg him to cooperate with my parents. He would look at me helplessly and say, "I just can't."

After he was arrested for stealing a movie banner of a scantily clad woman advertising *Gypsy*, my parents sent him away to boarding school. I pleaded with them not to do this, but they didn't listen.

The night before he left, I sat by him all evening, holding his hand and crying. I worried about him, only fifteen and off to a harsh school named Kemper Military Academy. I didn't see how emotionally I could let him go.

The next morning after breakfast, Jake carried his small suitcase to the car. He waved to me as he got into the back seat. I didn't wave back, but I looked at his face. I tried to memorize it because I knew I wouldn't see him for a long time. My dad drove him away.

People were always coming and going in my family. Soon after Jake left, Dad left too. He moved to a town three hours away to work in a hospital and came home about once a month. I was glad my dad left, but Jake was another matter.

I cosseted myself with literature. Reading soothed me, kept me occupied, and entertained me. It filled me with a sense of purpose and educated me about the world and myself. Reading is surely one of the great gifts of life. When we have something to read, we are never lonely.

I read in my bedroom on the second floor with its east- and south-facing windows. The mahogany desk beside my bed held my papers and pens and my diary. I had two bookcases full of books and a tall pile on the floor. In warm weather I would read outside on a blanket on the grass, but in cooler months, I would lie on my bed, a big book in my hands, and disappear into a world far from the one I lived in, luxuriating in my light-filled room and the light-filled space the book and I created together.

The A&W on Highway 81

When I was fourteen, I interviewed to work at the A&W on Highway 81. The owner, Melvin Thune, was a balding, portly man whom I considered old, but who was probably in his fifties. He asked only my age and my grade point average. During our interview he barely made eye contact, and when he told me I was hired, I could hardly hear him.

I started work the next day for fifty-five cents an hour plus tips. My shifts were four P.M. to eleven P.M. five days a week, from May through September. I rarely saw Melvin at the A&W again. He worked from home and turned much of the day-to-day management of the drive-in over to us high school students.

The A&W was in a small building with a ledged window for us carhops, and a front room that housed the ice, coffee pots, ice cream, and drink machines. Behind that front room was the kitchen, filled with freezers, fryers, stacks of buns, and vats of ketchup, mustard, mayo, lettuce, pickles, and onions.

We carhops wore black slacks, checkered orange and black shirts, and black leather aprons that held our order books, pens, and money. We served twenty carports, ten on each side of a long runway. At each port was a box with a shiny menu offering everything from tuna melts to root beer floats. When a car drove in, we would give the occupants a few minutes to look at the menu, then we would briskly walk down the runway to take the order and collect the money.

A few minutes later, we would deliver a tray filled with sandwiches, hot and cold drinks, fries or onion rings. We hooked the tray to the open window of the car door and then retired until the driver flashed his or her headlights, signaling it was time to clear away the tray.

This work further schooled me in the behavior of the human race. All kinds of people came to that A&W. Tired truckers, lonely old bachelors, farmworkers, young men in training at the nearby National Guard Armory, and other teenagers, sometimes on dates, but more likely cruising with their friends.

I learned how to deal with flirtatious men and stingy and persnickety people. I challenged myself to win people over and to really get to know them. Soon I had regular customers I loved to see. They were the smilers and jokers or the ones who beamed friendliness my way.

Some couples were so kind to each other that I could almost believe in true love. I also saw sneering, patronizing husbands with sullen wives, or couples who were totally silent with each other, as if they were separate ice cubes at far ends of a tray. Some parents joked with their children and created a happy atmosphere; others bossed the kids around sufficiently to ruin even a trip for ice cream. Still other families had children who were totally in control and badgering their parents for more, more, more.

Every now and then, I would sense that I was dealing with an abusive man. I could tell by looking at the wives' and children's frightened faces. In one terrible family, the parents drove up in an old clunker and ordered two large chocolate ice cream cones. They sat in the front seat eating those big cones, with their hungry-eyed children in the back silently watching.

I liked observing as I worked, and I liked my regular customers. My people skills improved, I had interesting conversations, and I became more organized. All the way through college, I continued to do restaurant work. From this work, I learned many lessons I would later use as a therapist. I had practice dealing with indecisive, grumpy, or persnickety people. I learned to be cheerful with all types of people.

I also learned how much I love to work. As a child, I had always assigned myself work, such as baking mud pies for my mother or learning new vocabulary words, and I had loved working in my mom's clinic after school. But with the A&W, I realized that work would always be one of my favorite parts of life.

When I was sixteen, Melvin promoted me to chief cook and manager. As a carhop, my tips had been good, and with my promotion, my pay actually diminished. Over time I learned the multiple skills one needs to turn out large amounts of food in a short amount of time. The girls who worked at the A&W weren't difficult to supervise. We liked our jobs and got along well. After I became manager, Melvin let me recommend who to hire.

In the kitchen I was totally in charge. On busy nights I had one or two helpers to whom I would assign tasks, such as pulling more onion rings out of the freezer or refilling the condiment vats. But I was the cook, flipping the burgers, deep-fat frying the pork tenderloins, and lifting fries out of the hot corn oil to drain. On slow nights, I played music and practiced my dance moves. I snacked the nights away. In a health code violation that I dare confess to only now, I often dipped dill pickles in ketchup straight from the big vat. I also made myself floats of coffee and soft-serve and ate an average of three fish sandwiches every night.

Perhaps I should note here that I liked Melvin Thune. He was a shy man, but he was kind and respectful to all the girls who worked at the A&W. His business model seemed casual, but it actually worked. He hired only workers with above a B average, and then he left us alone to do the right thing. In spite of his rare appearances, he had few personnel problems and the place was clean and efficient. The only health code violation was my own eating of dill pickles dipped in ketchup. We staff felt well treated, and Melvin made enough money to go to Vegas for a month every January.

I enjoyed being a carhop on a blistering Saturday night. I would stand up front in the bright lights watching Highway 81 for that moment when the cars turned our way. I could hear the sounds of laughter and talking all around me and see the many insects illuminated golden by the headlights. At the right moment, I walked down the bright runway, lights flashing all around me, to step up to the driver's window and ask, "Your order, please."

The work I did at the A&W taught me a great deal about the world and myself. First jobs can be important for building identity. Through our new insights and the reflected appraisals of the world we develop a sense for who we are.

The world seemed less complicated then. I was making straight A's and had a scholarship to the University of Kansas. I had friends, a good job, and faith that my future was going to be exciting. I had dreams, contradictory dreams. I might wander the world like Tolstoy's pilgrim, or I might be an editor in New York City and drink champagne. But I had all the confidence of the young that I could make my dreams come true.

Now I know that none of us can make all of our dreams come true. We don't have enough time, talents, or good luck. And choices close as well as open possibilities. I have never lived in New York City and instead have spent most of my life in Nebraska. But I've had a richer life than I could have dreamed of when I was watching for headlights at the A&W.

San Francisco

By my senior year, my parents were proud of me. I had always been the golden girl who made good grades, took care of my younger siblings, and was polite and friendly with everyone. In addition, I was the confidante of both of my parents. In December of that year, I was invited into a special honors program at the university and given a scholarship. My parents decided to reward me by taking me on a trip to San Francisco. That was their favorite place, and they wanted to share it with me. As usual, my dad drove nonstop to our destination. We made it from Kansas to San Francisco in thirty hours.

I remember coming into the Bay Area and being astounded by the light, which was so sparkly on the green hills with their rows of pastel houses. Later in the day, when the fog rolled in, I couldn't believe it. It seemed like a miraculous phenomenon that only the most fortunate people would be allowed to witness.

We stayed at a hotel on Union Square, and I spent a lot of time there observing the street people and the Beats, who were playing drums and flutes, reading poetry, and passing out flyers. I yearned to be one of the people reading poetry in the square and determined that someday I would return.

A friend of mine who was in college had told me to make sure that my parents took me to North Beach and City Lights Bookstore. My parents agreed to do that the last day of our trip. But first, they wanted to show me their favorite old haunts. We rode a cable car to Fisherman's Wharf and walked along the bay to ward the Presidio. My parents talked nonstop, and their faces glowed with excitement.

We sat down on a bench for a while and looked at the sailboats and little ships in the bay. The Golden Gate Bridge shone in the afternoon sun. The city behind us seemed like a storybook city, a magic kingdom, where every dream could be realized, as we did the things my parents had loved to do. We ate lobsters on a red and white plastic tablecloth at Fisherman's Wharf, bought sourdough bread and good cheese for a picnic on Nob Hill, and stopped at See's Candies to buy what my mother described as the most delicious sweets in the world.

Both of my parents had been in the Navy. My father met my mother when he came to her office to shine her shoes. On their first date, he knew he wanted to marry her, but he waited to ask her until the third date. Both of them were high energy and spent every minute of their time off touring the city and having fun.

The second night we were there, we dined at their favorite restaurant from the war years. Omar Khayyam's was an elegant restaurant owned by a man who had survived the Armenian genocide. The lights were low and the thick linen tablecloth was set with beautiful plates and silverware. A lone gardenia was in a silver vase. I had never smelled one before and was dizzy from its perfume. The water glasses were so heavy that I joked I might not be strong enough to lift mine. We ordered foods I had never tasted: shish kebab, dolma, and pilaf. As we dined on this exotic meal, my parents almost seemed in love with each other.

Our last full day in the city we spent in Chinatown. My father paid for a street artist to sketch a charcoal picture of me. I bought little gifts for my siblings and friends, and we ate at a fancy red and gold restaurant. Again, my parents displayed their sophistication by ordering egg foo young, chop suey, and General Tso's chicken. My mother taught me how to eat with chopsticks.

After this wonderful lunch, my parents accompanied me to North Beach. The streets were filled with barefoot men with long hair and thin women in black, smoking cigarettes and talking about art. I was extremely embarrassed by my parents, who were chubby, smalltown Kansans, who did not know how to behave in a Bohemian environment. As if I did!

But inside City Lights bookstore, I forgot all about them. I picked up book after book of small press poetry. I read Allen Ginsberg's *Howl* and several poems from Lawrence Ferlinghetti's *Coney Island of the Mind*. There was a book by Anne Sexton, too, and one by Gary Snyder, and another by Gregory Corso. I had never been exposed to Beat poetry before, yet it deeply resonated with me. My parents stayed with me for a while and then went outside to sit on a bench and people-watch. From that bench they could see the developing strip clubs along Broadway and Columbus. Carol Doda, with her newly invented breast implants, was the star of the big new Condor Club. When I came out with my three poetry books, my mother said, "I'm glad this wasn't around when we were here." And my father said, "It was around, but you didn't know about it."

Then we went to a coffeehouse, called Coffee and Confusion, that I had been told about. The place was minimalist, with straw on a concrete floor and barefoot waiters. A young woman with long, blonde, iron-flattened hair was playing guitar and singing at the front of the room. Our handsome waiter, wearing only overalls and with his hair down to his waist, asked what we would like to order. To my incredible chagrin, my father asked for a martini. I wanted to melt into the floor with embarrassment. The waiter smirked a little bit and explained they only served coffee and tea.

That night, we had our final dinner at an Italian place in North Beach. As we sat in candlelight, I reflected on my relationship to my parents. I loved my mother, but she was so rarely around. I loved my father, too, but I had many memories of him behaving badly. I realized that, whatever their flaws, it would be hard for me to leave them and go to college. And it would be hard for them too. I felt like the glue that held our family together. I was the one they could always depend on to make things workable.

I had inherited their high energy levels, their curiosity, and their love of work, but I was very different from them too. My strong suit was empathy, and my deepest curiosity was about how people feel. Part of being ready to leave home is being able to see how we are like our parents and how we are different. We are even more ready when we don't make judgments about these differences.

As we talked over our lasagna dinner, I felt many things at once—my mother and father had created me and defined the landscape of my life. I had made choices and learned skills that allowed me to move through that landscape in a mostly happy way. At the end of the dinner, I lifted my glass of limeade and made a toast to my wonderful parents. My father began to cry.

V

Leaving Home

The Fiery Furnace

A week after high school graduation, my parents drove me to my new home in Corbin Hall at the University of Kansas. This event was so momentous that, except for a few cautions from my father about alcohol and premarital sex, we barely spoke on the way to Lawrence. I was jumpy with anxiety and excitement, and my parents were sad, really sad. I could see it on their drawn faces and pursed lips.

Before we went to my dorm, we drove around the campus. KU was a beautiful place, built on a series of hills overlooking downtown and the Kaw Valley. Old hardwoods shaded the lawns and the walkways. The buildings on campus were made of stone and covered with ivy. There was a gigantic library, an art gallery, a chapel, and a grand student union. KU looked exactly like we thought a college should look. We all had an almost religious belief in the sanctity of higher education, and everything we saw reinforced this vision.

We parked in front of the dorm and carried my luggage, blanket, and big dictionary up to my room on the second floor. Other students were in the lobby already, and I blushed with embarrassment at my nearby parents. At that time, many teenagers liked to pretend that we had sprung from the head of Zeus and constructed ourselves without parental influences.

When the unloading was finished and it was time to say goodbye, we stood around awkwardly in my new room. My family didn't hug, kiss, or speak about our emotions, and that left a small repertoire of behavior to draw from. Finally, we mumbled our goodbyes. My mother reminded me I could call long distance every Sunday night and talk for fifteen minutes. She added, "You can write every day if you have the time."

When the door closed behind them, I was left in an empty dormitory room, awaiting an unknown roommate. I was aware that I was at a portal ready to step into a new me, a new life. I had never felt so free. I could do whatever I wanted and be anyone I chose to be.

I had enrolled in an Honors program for students from all over the Midwest. We would live together and take small classes from professors in our fields of study. I wanted to be in the humanities programs, but my parents had insisted I sign up for the science section.

My roommate, Janice, showed up just before dinner. She was small with dark, curly hair and a button nose. We had our first cafeteria meal together and then talked all night in our dorm room. Janice was a big reader and deeply interested in politics and community organizing. As she talked about her life, I realized I was listening to someone like me. By morning, when we sleepily stumbled down to breakfast, I knew from that time on, my life would be different and bigger.

I wore nylons, a plaid jumper, and penny loafers to the first day of classes. I still was a conservative, small-town girl, eager to fit in, but that Mary lasted only a few weeks. Soon I was wearing jeans, beads, and a leather vest.

I barely remember my classes, but I recall vividly almost everything else. My new friends were mostly from big cities and much more sophisticated than I. Greg from St. Louis wore a tweed jacket with a peyote button on it and liked to quote existential philosophers. Rob, another student from Kansas City, was openly gay. Wayne played jazz saxophone and praised John Coltrane and Gerry Mulligan. Janice was dating Tom, who had applied to be a conscientious objector, and they were participating in civil rights and antiwar marches.

Opportunities were everywhere. The foreign film theater showed movies by Bergman, Kurosawa, Buñuel, and Fellini. The art gallery was filled with classical and modern art. The Union had biweekly programs with famous artists like Odetta, Allen Ginsberg, and Buffy Sainte-Marie. Like my mother, I almost gave up sleep. I didn't want to miss anything.

My favorite spot was in a church basement just a few blocks from campus. The Fiery Furnace was open every Friday and Saturday night from eight to midnight. In my first month of school, Greg invited me to come with him to the Friday night hootenanny and poetry reading. We walked down some dimly lit stairs into a large room. Except for the spotlight on the stage, the only light sources were the tall candles in wine bottles on every table.

I ordered a coffee for the first time in my life. The flickering lights, the smell of fresh ground beans, and all the students talking at nearby tables made the whole scene magical.

That night had three different events. The first was a barefoot young woman with silver-gold hair who played a lute and sang English ballads in a beautiful soprano voice. The next was poetry; young men all thin and dressed in black took turns reading their angry verse. Their hair was below their ears, long by the standards of the day, and they wore sandals rather than the Oxfords or loafers that most men wore. The last man to read had a guitar and a bass player accompany him as he recited a kind of syncopated intense poetry. Even though I didn't have the courage to speak to him, I fell hard for this poet and had dreams in which he would ask me for a date.

The third event was a jazz band. I knew jazz from my dad—Glenn Miller, Count Basie, and Ella Fitzgerald—but this was different. The music was jerkier, harder to follow with more of a mood than a melody. I didn't understand the music, but I wanted to. I determined to ask Wayne to lend me some modern jazz records so I could study it.

Soon I, too, was marching for civil rights in Kansas City. I opposed the war in Vietnam and joined the girls in my dorm in opposition to the university's *in loco parentis* policies and curfews for young women. I could talk about modern poetry and European filmmakers with the other students. I could tell a Manet from a Monet.

I thought I was totally free in those early days on campus, but I was wrong. I missed my family terribly. When I called home the first few weeks of college, all I could do was cry into the phone. I didn't want to return to Concordia. But, despite my free-spirited persona, I loved my family desperately, and the pain of being separated echoed with all the other separations over the years.

I changed my politics and my personal habits and I felt self-created, but that was an eighteen-year-old's illusion. I still carried within me my parents, my grandparents, and all of my aunts, uncles, and cousins. I carried my family traumas, the little towns I had lived in, the Methodist Church, the books I had read. Mrs. Van Cleave, Jeanie, and the Concordia sandpit were with me.

My magpie Maggie, the baby coyotes, the slaughtered rabbit pets, and Pixie Rosarita were all there too. I walked into the Fiery Furnace with the Bray and Page family genetics and my own odd dappled-light personality. I wasn't sure what would happen next in this turbulent world of the university in the mid-1960s, but I was ready.

Campfire Lights

By my second year at KU, many things had changed. Early mornings, I walked downtown to wait tables on the breakfast shift at Keim's Café. I had moved out of the dorm and into a room in the home of an older lady who rented to female students. Jake had left high school and joined my friends and me in Lawrence. And I had met my first serious boyfriend, Larry Ben Franklin. He was a tall, dark-eyed man who dressed in workingmen's clothes and boots and reminded me of a young Marlon Brando. Larry had dropped out of college to work as a union organizer at the local box factory.

I had settled in with a group of adventurous outsiders committed to art and freedom. Jeanine was a beautiful, sensual woman from Wichita who aspired to be an opera singer. Her best friend Dixie, also from Wichita, was a poet and artist who excelled at salty language and ribald wit. Jane from Kansas City was a sophisticated woman who seemed both deeply cynical and highly amused by the comedy of life that unfurled before her. She chain-smoked and, in her husky voice, made frequent droll remarks. Even at eighteen, she seemed world-weary.

How we could talk! Our conversations ranged from Marxism to Sufism, Taoism, phenomenology, and politics. We discussed civil rights, human rights, Kabuki theater, the beat poets, and music and art. We lent each other paperback copies of Alan Watts, Malcolm X, and Simone de Beauvoir, and we talked endlessly about the ideas of our times. We stayed up late discussing things as if when we finally figured out our positions, we would be ready to change the world.

Meanwhile, we had studies or jobs or both. Jake worked construction. Jane dropped out of school and worked as a secretary. Dixie and Jeanine dropped out too. I stayed in and ploughed diligently through my premed courses. I luxuriated in the elective courses that I was free to choose—Russian history, art history, music history, Spanish, and French.

Sometimes Larry and I visited the Nelson Art Gallery in Kansas City. Then he would drive us to a juke joint along the Missouri River where we could eat barbecue and listen to James Brown and Aretha Franklin. Once, when he had had several beers, Larry jumped on top of our table and declared Aretha Franklin "Queen of the World."

Other nights we would hit the late-night clubs around 18th and Vine. This area was the birthplace of the Kansas

City style of jazz. Count Basie, Charlie Parker, and Coleman Hawkins were from Kansas City. Larry and I followed Jay McShann, Claude Williams, and the Scamps with Earl Robinson. Before these experiences with music and the marches, my world had been almost exclusively white.

Our group held parties lit by candles and fueled by red wine. Usually these parties were in big old houses that many students shared. The living room would be for dancing, the kitchen would have the wine and a big pot of chili or lentil soup, and all the other rooms would be for talking, the most popular activity. All of us were exploding with ideas that we felt compelled to share. We made plans to write books, to organize communal farms, and to perform street theater. These parties lasted until dawn. Afterward, we would walk down to Keim's Café for breakfast.

Our group traveled together to concerts in Kansas City or Topeka. Once we piled in the back of a pickup and sat on bales of straw for a ride to Lincoln to hear Bob Dylan with Mike Bloomfield. Dylan's new electric music absolutely stunned us. We had expected a quiet, soulful concert, and instead the stage was on fire with crazy energy. A few people in the crowd booed, but we loved it. On the way home in the bumpy old pickup, we sang songs under the stars.

We had picnics and potlucks or took turns cooking communal meals. I remember one meal in particular cooked by Larry's best friend, a Danish filmmaker named Pym. He said he had come to America in hopes of dating Mouseketeer Annette Funicello, but instead he found himself in Lawrence, Kansas, studying film and living with his girlfriend, Lydia. Pym peeled a five-pound bag of potatoes and chopped up five yellow onions and two long coils of baloney. Then he fried it all up in a giant skillet. Delicious.

My favorite summer activity was our weekend outings to Lone Star Lake, a large, clear lake surrounded by cottonwoods and oaks. Our group knew an isolated spot with a swimming beach, a horseshoe pit, and a fire ring. After swimming or clowning around with beach balls or horseshoes, Jeanine and Dixie would teach us simple folk dances and sing as we swayed and whirled in a circle.

Later, we gathered branches for a fire and soon had a roaring blaze. We roasted hot dogs and opened cans of pork and beans. All of us were poor, and on a lucky night, somebody would have sprung for a can of black olives or some grapes. And someone always had a guitar for songs around the fire. We would sing "'Tis a Gift to Be Simple," "This Land Is Your Land," "Hard Times Come Again No More," "Mr. Tambourine Man," and "Turn! Turn! Turn!"

Larry and I sat close together and passed a bottle of Boone's Farm between us. We were crazy for each other, and if we touched or looked into each other's eyes, we melted with desire. Together we watched the fire, listened to the wind in the trees, and looked to the sky for shooting stars. Occasionally we would hear a barn owl or a nighthawk.

The echo of the campfire shimmered on the lake's surface. Sometimes moonlight also illuminated the sky and flashed its glow across the lake toward us. We were happy with life and each other, and we believed this life of ours would go on forever. Instead it was as ephemeral as a meteor shower.

Dock of the Bay

My sophomore year in college, one happy thing and three sad things happened to me. The happy thing was my brother fell in love with my friend Jeanine. The sad things were my like-minded roommate, Janice, and her boyfriend quietly slipped out of the country to avoid the draft. Janice couldn't even say goodbye. That same semester my father had a severe stroke, and, second semester, Larry became mentally ill.

Thanksgiving morning, Larry drove Jake and me to Concordia. He hadn't met my parents or siblings yet. Although Larry was polite and respectful, my Dad didn't like him. Perhaps it was because of Larry's leftist politics or the antiwar buttons on his jean jacket. More likely, it was because he saw Larry touching me in a way that signaled we were intimate. After a tense holiday meal, we drove back to Lawrence. Larry asked me what seemed like an odd question, "Why haven't you been angrier?"

I suspected he was commenting on the shouting and the chaos that was our family. My father was steaming with just-under-the-surface rage, my mother seemed stern and distant, and my siblings were adrift and detached. I couldn't answer Larry. I had no anger, only a deep yearning to believe my family was okay and that we loved each other.

The next day, Mother called about noon to tell me Dad had suffered a debilitating stroke and was in a coma, unlikely to survive. Jake and I raced back home for a few desperate days. After seventy-two hours our father came to, but he was paralyzed on his right side, partially blind, and unable to do anything but grunt. He was only fifty, but his normal life was over.

I held myself accountable for this. I felt that my relationship with Larry inflicted so much stress on Dad that he had this stroke. I believed I had disappointed my father to the point of destroying him.

Eventually, I went back to school to finish the semester and take my finals. I left my mother alone to financially support the family, deal with my father, and care for my siblings. I finished the semester in a state of shock. I have no memory of it at all.

At Christmas break, I rode the train to Denver to stay with my dad at the Craig Hospital. Every day a speech therapist came in to help him relearn language, something he was never able to fully accomplish. Later, another therapist would put him in a wheelchair and haul him out for some exercises. In his hospital gown, he would stand between two bars balancing with his one good arm and leg. He tried to hurl his heavy, wounded body forward in what looked like a mockery of walking. Or he would try to touch his nose, and his hand would drift off in the wrong direction.

Gradually, he regained some speech, but it didn't match his thoughts. His main word was "cigarette," which he said when he wanted a glass of water, a teaspoon of soft food, or a bedpan. His other main words were "shit," "goddammit," and "coffee."

My dad was conscious enough to know how damaged he was, and at one point, he begged me to kill him. He pulled on his pillow with his left hand. I understood that he wanted me to smother him. I told him I couldn't do it. I secretly agreed with him that he would be happier dead, but I didn't have the courage to act. We both cried at my refusal.

At the end of semester break, I left him alone at the hospital and rode the train back to Lawrence. I was relieved to be heading to Larry and my classes, but I was also ashamed of myself for leaving Dad behind. I considered dropping out of school, but instead, I immersed myself in my studies and my friends.

My father stayed another six weeks in Denver. Then my Uncle Clair and Aunt Agnes picked him up and drove him back to Concordia. I saw him at spring break. He remained half blind, paralyzed on one side, and unable to say much beyond his four original words. He sat on our couch in the living room and called out demands, "Cigarette, Goddammit."

"Dad, you already are smoking a cigarette," I would respond. "Do you mean you want a glass of water?"

He would shake his head no and swear. I would ask, "Do you want your walker?"

That second semester, Larry began to hear voices and booked an appointment with a psychiatrist who prescribed medications for psychosis. The drugs made him stiff and slow. He talked to me about things that hadn't happened. I had no idea how to respond.

I wondered if Larry's problems were in any way related to our relationship. And I was overwhelmed by the feeling that my father had somehow suffered because of me. I felt that I was responsible for both men's well-being. At the same time, I knew that I didn't have the agency to take good care of them. I was only eighteen and numb with pain myself.

I decided to leave Lawrence. If I had invited him, Larry would have come with me, but I wanted to break up. I loved him, but I was terrified of his mental illness. I told myself I wanted to be free of encumbrances, but really, I was just afraid and on the run from my commitments.

At the end of the school year, I moved home for the summer to help my father with his speech therapy and physical exercises. I steadied him as he dragged his body back and forth across our living room. I held up cards with pictures, and Dad attempted to name the object. When I showed him a peach, he said, "Cigarette." When I showed him a car, he said, "Coffee." When I showed him a tree, he said, "Shit."

As we engaged in this frustrating process, I could hardly stand to look at my sad father with his twisted face, his right arm curled up over his chest, and his despairing eyes. But that summer I did keep him company. At least I did that.

Jake, Jeanine, and Dixie all moved to San Francisco that summer of 1967. The following spring, I joined them in a communal flat on Potrero Hill. Young people from all over the country had congregated there to discover their true identities and be part of the great youth movement of the times.

At that time, the city was a constant party. The streets were filled with colorful characters performing music or experimental theater, handing out oranges or roses, or distributing leaflets or invitations to readings and art shows. Golden Gate Park was the site of free concerts by Janis Joplin and Big Brother and the Holding Company, Jefferson Airplane, Country Joe and the Fish, and the Grateful Dead.

Dancing at the Fillmore or the Avalon Ballroom or picnicking at a happening on Mount Tamalpais, I tried to forget everything I had left behind. I immersed myself in the flow of energy, creativity, and hope.

Later, things in the Bay Area changed. Guns, hard drugs, and sociopaths became more prevalent. However, there was a time when the city was just pulsing with joy and goodwill. And I was part of its great heartbeat.

On sunny days, the light in San Francisco bounced off the blue bay and green hills. When the sun rose above a fog bank, the sky turned magenta and tangerine. The Golden Gate Bridge sparkled like a bronze sash above the bay dotted with white sails and the tourist boats to Alcatraz. On cloudy days, mother-of-pearl light radiated from the oyster of sky. Almost every morning the fog slowly dispersed across the seven hills of the city and paraded back over those same hills late in the afternoon. It seemed a living creature, as predictable as breath.

North Beach was filled with the garish lights of night-clubs and the illuminated stripper signs. Chinatown was ablaze in lanterns and colored lights. The city was a feast of light—water light, sky light, skyscraper light, cable car light, psychedelic light, and reflected light bouncing off yet more light.

For a while I lived communally with my brother and our friends. Later I had a small place on Fillmore Street in what was then a Black community. I worked at Dunkin' Donuts on Market Street, just across from the bus terminal that dumped out the troops arriving home from Vietnam. The flower children also arrived there from cities all over the country. Our donut shop was surrounded by peep shows and the Tenderloin District. All kinds of people came in to drink coffee and have a maple bar or chocolate donut. Even though I was the only waitress there, I had plenty of time to talk to my customers. I heard compelling stories every day.

San Francisco was a feast for the senses, with its smells of fish, bay water, and the sweaty bodies of workers and vagabonds. North Beach smelled of bourbon, cheap perfume, cigarettes, and the fresh bread of the Italian bakeries. Chinatown smelled like bok choy, roast duck, fish, and sesame oil. The Haight emanated patchouli, pot, coffee, and nicotine.

I had never lived near Asians, Blacks, or Latinos before. I became friendly with my Black neighbors, the Chicano man who sold soft tacos on the corner, and the topless activist by the laundromat passing out flyers on "Free Love." Even then I knew that was an oxymoron.

Every day was full of discoveries. One evening, Jake and I drove Mose Allison home from a jazz gig. Another time the poet Richard Brautigan bought me a cup of coffee and tried to pick me up. I had been warned about him and said, "No, thank you." I read poetry off the racks at City Lights, then managed by Ferlinghetti, and spent lazy sunlit afternoons at Ocean Beach. I learned to give Tarot readings and do Sufi dances. My friends and I camped at Big Sur and hiked at Point Lobos on weekend afternoons.

At the time, I would have said I was having fun and learning about the world. That's partly the truth. I was living in the center of the center of the universe having experiences I couldn't have even imagined a few years earlier. But I also had forsaken Larry and my father and the rest of my family in Kansas. When I slowed down enough to think about them, I was overwhelmed with sorrow and guilt. I felt like a coward and a deserter. I just hadn't been able to face the heartbreak at home.

Most of the time, I kept my anguish buried, but there was one night in particular that stands out. It was a few months after Otis Redding died in December 1967. His song "Dock of the Bay" was all over the airwaves. I was obsessed with that song and played it constantly on the turntable in my head. On March 11, my mother's birthday, I rode a cable car to a pier and sat looking at the water.

It was a clear, calm evening. The air was silky, and an almost full moon floated silver on the water. Thinking about Otis Redding's song made me sad, and soon I was crying, first for his loneliness and my own, but then for everything. I cried for my overworked, heartbroken mother, my lonely siblings, and my crippled father who sat in our house alone smoking and looking out the window. I cried for Larry who still wrote me every week. My heart ached from the hardness of it all. I could neither avoid suffering nor avoid inflicting it.

I mourned for the girl I had lost, the Mary who was a good daughter who was present for her family and eager to care for them. I was no longer that girl and I could never be her again. I didn't know who I was becoming.

As I looked at the moon, my heart felt as if it were breaking in many ways at once. I had come to San Francisco to find myself, but I was as lost as a person could be. What had looked like freedom felt like just a shiny bauble. I no longer knew what the word *freedom* meant. I wasn't even sure it was important. Maybe something else was more important, something I could call integrity.

The colored lights on the water reminded me of my father on a dock long ago in Texas. I was awash in emotion—in love with the city, mourning for Otis Redding, homesick as hell, and filled with a yearning for something I couldn't even name. My own sense of self was as fragile and floaty as the reflection of moonlight on water.

That night, the moonlight on the bay, the rocking of the ships in harbor, and the reflected lights from Fisherman's Wharf held no answers. The scene was beautiful, and it kept my shredded heart in place, but it could not illuminate a path forward.

Pregnancy and Exile

After my time in the city, I moved to Berkeley and graduated from there in the spring of 1969. Yet I remained rootless. I tried the world of office work and hated it. I barely tolerated wearing nylons and high heels, shuffling paper when I wanted to be outside, and spending time doing work I didn't value. When I received my first paycheck, I left for Mexico.

I lived alone in a little cabana for the summer on my paycheck and graduation money. On my twenty-first birthday, I flew Icelandic Air to London. I found work as a countergirl at a Jewish bakery. The two women owners were kind, relaxed, and easily amused. They had been through the war in London, and the 1960s didn't rattle them in the least. Indeed, their tolerance and laughter, as well as their delicious breads and pastries, kept the bakery crowded with customers.

I spent my free time drinking tea, walking around the city, and exploring the British Museum. After nine months, I was so homesick that I returned to Kansas. I was weary of poverty and rootlessness, and I committed myself to settling down.

After a few weeks with my family, I moved to Kansas City and enrolled in the last classes I needed for medical school. Soon I was taking advanced physics and organic chemistry at the University of Missouri.

Oh, and I became pregnant by a man I didn't want to marry. I had met him in my science classes, and at first, we had fun together, but over time he became more possessive and controlling and that scared me away.

The fall and winter of my pregnancy were among the hardest times of my life. My mother was ashamed and didn't want me to come home, even for the holidays. I had been afraid of exile years earlier when I bit the doctor before my surgery, but now I really was in exile. Furthermore, 1971 was not a time to be a single parent. Most people considered women like me loose and immoral.

I was broke, lonely, and vulnerable. I didn't have any maternity dresses or even a winter coat. Kansas City was dreary and cold, and I slopped around in old shoes and a shabby jacket.

For my medical school interview, I wore a borrowed loose-fitting jumper that hid my pregnancy. After I was accepted, I rode the bus to the UMKC campus every morning and struggled through my courses.

The doctor I found worked at the medical school and took me on as a charity case. This was when doctors still treated their colleagues for free, and I was on my way to being a colleague.

I was close to being homeless when my friend Dixie, who had returned from San Francisco, invited me to live with her family and friends in their large house near the Plaza.

About ten of us shared this old-fashioned house with a fireplace. We were all poor, but we had books, guitars, and the companionship of each other. In the evening, I helped Dixie cook meals of rice and beans or pasta and vegetables for a large table of friends. The guys did the dishes, and most of the time our beverage for the evening was tea made from alfalfa.

Dixie and I and her daughters made homemade decorations for Christmas and wrapped small presents for each other in newspaper.

Around the holidays, beautiful, fun-loving Laura showed up at our house. She had traveled with a boyfriend to the tip of South America and back. Now she was in Kansas City, broke and without her boyfriend. She had stored her belongings with Dixie and her husband, Fred. I had never met Laura, but I had been wearing her clothes. When she arrived, I was dressed in that same plaid jumper that I had worn to my medical school interview.

It was her jumper. Mercifully, she was amused by my "borrowing her stuff." Soon we were close friends. After the holidays, Laura found a waitress job at House of Toy on the Plaza. She and I moved into a small apartment just four blocks away. I was sleeping poorly, heavy with the baby, and schlepping through ice and snow to a bus stop to wait for a ride to school. I was in class or in labs all day and returned around sunset to an empty apartment. Most nights my stomach ached from hunger as I waited for Laura to come home with leftovers from the House of Toy.

She would arrive with bags of eggrolls and crab Rangoon and boxes of sweet and sour pork or orange chicken. Thanks to the generous Toy family, we would have our feast.

Once again, I found myself being saved by women friends who were present through my tough times. Without them, I can't imagine what would have become of me. They were my light in that dark winter.

Sunrise

In early March my mother called to say she would like to be present for the delivery. I was deeply relieved that she was coming back into my life and grateful she would be a doctor on the scene when my child was born. I wondered if she was still angry with me. I felt no anger toward her, only a deep sense of letting her down. I had stopped being a golden child quite a while ago.

By late March, on a Friday afternoon, with a week of spring break coming, my baby decided it was time. How thoughtful he was to arrive when I had a whole week free of school and studies!

I called my mother three hours away, and Laura and I took a taxi to the hospital. The nurse who examined me said my doctor was out to dinner and would check on me later. Laura stayed by my side, offering me ice chips and making hospital jokes.

At ten the doctor showed up with alcohol on his breath. But he was kind and professional as he examined me. He said I was doing fine and he would come back in a few hours. My mother rushed in around midnight. As the labor became more painful, she and Laura stayed by my side.

I was shocked by the pain. I had always had a high pain threshold, but this was pain on a different level. Why hadn't anyone warned me? I remember thinking I would like to stop the process and just spend a few more days preparing to have a baby. Then I realized, of course, that I wasn't in control of when that baby would be born. My only choice was to go forward as bravely as I could.

I breathed in and out, deeply and slowly. I clutched Laura's hand and looked toward my mother for comfort. She kept her eyes on the fetal heart monitor. At some point, she said the baby and I could come to Concordia for the summer. At another point, she offered to keep the baby for me until I graduated from medical school. I was horrified by that. I couldn't imagine ever wanting to be separated from my baby, even for one day. Mother didn't know me very well. This baby wasn't just in my family, he was part of me.

This offer was emblematic of the way my mother thought. She was pragmatic and believed you could arrange a family according to what worked best in the practical sense. She did not understand attachment the way most people do.

About five A.M. things happened fast. My doctor arrived, my mother donned a surgical gown, and I was wheeled into the operating room. The lights were bright, the table was cold and hard, and I began pushing. Someone gave me a shot. I heard a baby cry. My mother said, "It's a boy."

The next thing I remember is being back in my hospital room. Laura and my mother had gone to our apartment to rest. I was groggy, sore, and hungry. I wanted my baby.

Soon, a nurse carried in my son. When she handed him to me, I looked into his eyes. They were sky blue, clear and fresh, yet they also carried some knowledge of a universe I no longer remembered.

As I write this, I can still remember the feel of that warm swaddled baby in my arms and his soft blond hair, small shoulders, and long, bony feet. I could have stayed in that room alone with him forever.

Just then, the sun topped the horizon and rose until it burst golden through the window. The light flowed over us like an embrace. Together we were held by that light, a Pietà in a Kansas City hospital with a broke, unemployed mother and sacred baby son. I named my son Ezekiel Sunrise. I knew I would give my life for him. More to the point, I would grow up for him.

Fireplace Light

In the summer of 1972, I drove to Lincoln to search for a graduate program. The anthropology department accepted me but could offer no financial support. On impulse, I crossed a green lawn and visited the psychology department in Burnett Hall. The director of the clinical psychology program was a soft-spoken southerner named James Cole. By a miracle of good luck, he was free.

We talked for a couple of hours. He looked over my transcripts and test scores, and then offered me a fully funded place in the clinical training program. I floated back to my car almost in shock from such a stunning act of generosity. Zeke and I now had a future.

On the first day of class I found myself standing outside Dr. Cole's office with a tall, slim man who looked like a Native American. He was dressed in jeans, a western shirt, and cowboy boots. His long hair was pulled back in a ponytail.

As we waited, I introduced myself and chatted excitedly about classes. Jim answered in dour monosyllables. Later I learned he had won "Best Singer" at a music festival the night before. He had hardly slept, and his interest in graduate school was limited. He hoped to be a full-time musician soon. Psychology was only his fallback plan.

The next day Zeke and I attended the faculty and graduate student picnic at the Unitarian Church. It was a sunny afternoon, and Zeke was excited by the playground equipment. I looked happily at the potluck table filled with foods I couldn't afford—fried chicken, ham, and a fresh strawberry pie. The students were from all over the country and every ethnic group. My class included Jim, a nun, two African Americans from the South, and two Latinos. Some of the students were married and had children for Zeke to befriend.

I was a unique student—an unmarried mother, a Berkeley graduate, and entirely new to the field of psychology. Furthermore, I looked like a hippie with my miniskirt, leather vest, and headband. The students were friendly, but some of the faculty were alarmed. I could tell by their questions that they were checking me out.

Zeke wanted to play on the swings, and Jim offered to take him. That left me free to talk to other students and my professors. I took the opportunity to reassure faculty members that I was a serious student who could handle graduate school and single parenting. I had a wonderful time at the picnic. Psychologists are by nature kind, empathic, and observant. The students seemed like just the people I would choose to spend the next four years with.

Zeke had his share of attention too. He was a lively, extroverted eighteenth-month-old, and people kept giving him cookies and picking him up for hugs. I couldn't recall a time I had had more fun and met a more interesting group of people. I felt grateful to Jim for giving me time to talk to others.

It turns out Jim only looked like a Native American. He was a German American whose family homesteaded in Burt County along the Missouri River. Early on, our small class of clinical psychology students decided to have study sessions together for statistics. This weed-out course was taught by an old Czech who had been a mathematician in World War II. He was a brilliant statistician but a terrible teacher. Graduate-level statistics with its probability theory, research methods, and ANOVA was tough slogging. Our weekly sessions met at my apartment at eight P.M. after Zeke went to sleep.

I lived in one of two apartments on the first floor of a three-story rundown house on A Street. An old couple named Millie and Ray lived across the hall from me. On the rare occasions I went out at night, they watched Zeke for me. My furnished apartment had a porch onto the side yard, a living and dining room, one bedroom, and a bath. Its great luxury was an elegant old fireplace in the living room. I managed to buy firewood so I could study beside the fire.

As the first semester proceeded, Jim did well in statistics, and he explained it to the rest of us. I didn't have the best math mind in the world, and I was neither confident about nor interested in the subject. I needed extra tutoring, and Jim stayed afterward to help me. The first time this happened, we both made it clear we were only study buddies and would never date each other. That would make our lives way too complicated.

Jim was reflective, perceptive, and funny. Before our tests, he would write the phone number of a truck-driving school on the blackboard and say, "Remember, folks, we have alternatives." In the student room, he had us all laughing with his spot-on imitations of our professors. Sometimes when my seventy-five-dollar Karmann Ghia wouldn't start, he would give Zeke a ride to the university preschool and me a ride to class.

I had vowed to stay single until I had my PhD. I was lucky to be in graduate school, and I wasn't going to let anything interfere with that. When I did date, I planned to be selective and cautious. I hoped my next relationship would lead to marriage and a father for Zeke. Jim was clearly not seeking a long-term commitment with anyone, and, of course, he didn't want to compromise his education either. He was also two years younger than me and a rock-and-roll musician. He hoped to tour the country with his band. So we made an easy deal, no dating.

That held through September, October, and November. Then, in December, our group had its last study session before finals. It was snowing hard outside and most people left early, but I was confused by covariance and I asked Jim to stay and help me. While he put another log on the fire, I poured us more coffee. With Zeke sleeping soundly in the next room, we worked side by side on the couch.

It was a lovely night. Outside, soft snow blanketed my porch and swirled around the Norway pines. I could see in the headlights of cars the rapidly falling snow. Occasionally the wind gusts rocked the creaky old house just enough to remind us how lucky we were to be inside. The cedar crackled in the glowing fire. The firelight danced across the room, lit Jim's face, and haloed his dark brown hair.

Sparks popped and glowed and not just in the fireplace. As I listened to Jim's patient, clear explanations, I found myself feeling attracted to him. I pushed back that forbidden feeling and kept studying. When our hands accidently touched, I felt as if I had touched the fire.

Finally, around eleven, Jim thought I understood covariance well enough to pass the final. After waking at five with Zeke and a long day of study, I was exhausted. Still, I considered inviting Jim to stay for a glass of wine. Given the way I was feeling, I didn't dare do that.

As Jim put on his heavy coat, he seemed to be hesitating to leave too. We both stood looking at the fire and at the white world beyond my window. My thoughts made me blush and that embarrassed me so much I blushed some more.

Jim had his hand on the doorknob, but he hadn't opened the door or called out his usual cheery goodbye. He kept his eyes on his cowboy boots and moved his books uneasily in his arms. Suddenly, I felt my heart racing and my throat go dry. I knew I was about to do something against my better judgment and dangerous to my career. But even as I felt imperiled, I felt impelled.

I looked directly at Jim and said, "I am starting to have non–study buddy feelings for you."

Jim looked up at me. I made a palms-up hopeless gesture and looked away in embarrassment. I felt I had blurted out the impermissible. Jim was silent for what seemed like a long time. When I finally looked into his face, I could tell he was struggling with my statement. I feared I had put him on the spot.

Finally, he said gruffly, "Dammit, so am I."

We both laughed at how frustrated he sounded. I invited him to stay for a glass of wine and a conversation. We sat by the fire and talked through our situation. Both of us had a dozen reservations, but our careful words were at odds with our hormones. After an hour, we kissed each other good night. Not a study buddy kiss.

That night we couldn't have known that we would be together for more than fifty years. We couldn't have anticipated the conflicts, the ups and downs, the challenges of our work and families, the moves, the travel, and our future careers in writing and music. We couldn't have envisioned the funeral parlors and cemeteries, the dying parents, or the chaos of 2020. Together we created a family that now includes twelve members and a community of friends. We've watched hundreds of swim meets and violin recitals, volleyball games, and soccer tournaments. We've traveled together for decades as I made speeches and conducted workshops. That night in December we were on the incandescent cusp of our future lives, and all we could see was the light, all we could feel was the heat.

My Father's Death

In April 1975, I endured the grueling comprehensive exams for my PhD. For six hours a day for a week, we were required to answer essay questions citing multiple research studies from memory. I had been studying for this test since January, and my parents knew I was worried. A fail on any part of it meant no PhD.

The day we received our results, Dad called to see if I had passed. With his shattered speech I could barely understand him, but I knew what he wanted to know. "Yes, Dad, I passed. I'll have my degree soon."

I could sense he wanted more details, but I had ordered pizza for a celebratory picnic with classmates and it was ready for pickup. "I'll talk to you later," I said, "I am in a hurry. Thanks for calling. I love you."

My dad said, "Cigarette, cigarette."

I knew that meant "I love you."

Four days later my mother called to say Dad had suffered another stroke. Jim, Zeke, and I drove down for the ICU vigil. All of my family except Jake were at the hospital. Soon he would be flying home from San Francisco. We camped in the emergency room waiting area and took turns going in to be with Dad.

The two days we spent there seemed to last forever. Mother looked grim and exhausted. We siblings didn't know what to say to each other. Small talk felt awkward, and we had no words to discuss the looming loss we were facing. We read, played gin rummy and Pitch, and waited for updates.

Meanwhile, Dad lay with an oxygen mask over his face. He was an odd bluish color and his hands felt cold and heavy, as if he were already dead. Various clear plastic bags emptied into a port on his shoulder. A catheter bag hung by the bed. Machines with blue, red, and white lights monitored his vitals. I watched the jumpy line representing his fast, irregular heartbeat.

The skin on his feet was dry and cracked, and I rubbed lanolin on his feet. I put my lips right up to his ear and thanked him for the summers of waterskiing and the trips to Mexico. I said I was happy that he knew Jim and Zeke. I told him I had a good life and I hoped he was proud of me. I couldn't honestly say he was a good father; he had damaged us children too much for that. Instead I said I knew he loved us and that we all loved him.

After the second night of our hospital campout, the doctors came at sunrise to say it was time to turn off our father's machines. They told us that he had no significant brain activity and would never wake again. We all looked at our mother's face. Her lips were pursed and she was shaking, but she nodded in agreement.

We gathered in the ICU cubicle to say one last goodbye. I wished Jake were with us, but he wouldn't arrive until evening. I asked if we could wait, but my mother and the other doctors were in charge.

The last few minutes I was with Dad, I hugged his head and shoulders and kissed his forehead. I remembered a story he had told me about leaving for Korea when I was three. I had been riding my tricycle in the yard, pretending indifference to his going. He came down the walk in his khakis carrying a heavy duffel bag. He bent low and asked for a goodbye kiss. He was crying, but my heart was hard. I looked him in the eyes and said, "You'll be sorry, Daddy."

Now I understood how sorry he had been that day. But today, I knew he would be glad to be leaving us. And I was happy for him. He was escaping painful years of being helpless and brain damaged.

I watched as the line on the heart monitor flattened and slowed until it was only a line and not a measurement of anything. RIP Frank Houston Bray, dead at fifty-nine.

We decamped from the waiting room and carried our blankets and books out of the hospital and into the morning sunlight. It seemed too bright outside, almost blinding. For two days, that waiting room had been our world. Now we didn't quite know what to do with this other world where daffodils and tulips were blooming and neighbors waved on their way to work.

I asked to be alone and walked the long way home. I was wrestling with a complicated sorrow.

Had my father died before he had his first stroke in 1967, I might have felt more anger toward him. After all, he had whipped my brothers, told me I wasn't pretty enough to find a husband, and repeatedly left us for long periods of time. But by the time he died, I had seen him endure unimaginable suffering. He could barely walk, talk, or see and was paralyzed on one side. He carried his right hand around with his left. He was in and out of rehab, sometimes recovering just enough for his progress to be wiped out by yet another stroke.

His old friends deserted him, and his family was rarely around. Sometimes he went for a little drive on his riding lawn mower. He tried one-handed cooking, but his timing was off, and after serving bloody chicken and uncooked beans a few times, he no longer tried to cook. He had to struggle to do everything. Walking up the stairs, eating, or conveying a thought—all these were so laborious. No, whatever anger I had bottled up over the years evaporated. I only felt love and sympathy.

My father had a short, hard life. After his father died, his mother raised three children during the Great

Depression in the poorest part of our country. She married seven times, and many of my dad's stepfathers beat him. He had scars on his feet from burns and injuries he had sustained going barefoot as a child.

Like Elvis, he never recovered from losing his mama. She had provided my dad with what stability and grounding he had. His wife was often unavailable, and his three older children all turned into what he considered hippies.

He was afraid of his own dark history. His grandfather had been mentally ill, and his own father had committed himself to the state mental hospital in Sedalia after the crash of the stock market in 1929 and stayed there all his life. Other relatives had also been mentally ill, and my dad was terrified he would lose his sanity. That fear for himself and for us children made him more than a little imbalanced.

My father was a better father than any of the men who raised him. No doubt he beat my brothers less than he had been beaten. He gave us what he never had—a house to live in, plenty of food, clothing, and toys.

His love language was admonishment. He criticized and lectured us constantly. He felt that if we made good grades and went to college, we would have economic security and we might be safe. He wanted John and me to be doctors and Jake to be a lawyer. Even though he had achieved none of these goals himself, he wanted us to have money, be respectable, and fit in with high-class people.

Of course, he had had fun, playing sports in high school and dating my mother during the war. Later, he enjoyed fishing on the Gulf Coast and driving our family to Yellowstone and the Black Hills. But he led a life of separation, from his families and from his own wounded heart.

It's easy to catalog my father's faults, but it's much harder to explain his virtues that were many but exercised only intermittently. He was a complicated man, greatly traumatized and filled with anger and fear. But he was also courageous, self-sacrificing, and fun-loving. He could be tender and gentle. He loved to take black-and-white pictures of birds and flowers. He had beautiful handwriting. Even in my seventies, I can't sum up my emotions about him. He was as even a mix of light and darkness as anyone I've ever known.

For many decades I believed I had caused his stroke by being against the Vietnam War and by bringing Larry home for Thanksgiving. I felt guilty that I had not helped Dad kill himself and that I had abandoned the family for San Francisco and Europe. Over the years, that guilt has softened. I didn't owe it to my father to adopt his political beliefs or abstain from sexual relationships. I am not sure even now that I could help anyone with euthanasia. I wish I had been more present for my family after Dad's stroke, but after a few years of rambling, I lived near my parents until they died.

At one time I would have said that the most complex relationships of my life were with my parents. I wouldn't say that now. My experience of being the parent of adult children has been equally complex, with the same mixtures of guilt and joy, attachment and loss, fear and love.

VI

Settling Down

The Fourth of July

When our children were young, we all had bicycles. Mornings, I rode mine to teach at the university, and then, at noon, I rode it to my therapy practice. Zeke and Sara cruised our neighborhood with their friends. After dinner in summer, we had family rides along Lincoln's many trails.

On the Fourth of July we rode our bikes through crowds of people to the fireworks on Holmes Dam. This was a major expedition. We carried a blanket, water bottles, and snacks for the evening. We weaved through cars, bikes, and pedestrians all heading in the same direction. The air was acrid with smoke, and the sidewalks and streets were streaked black from all the little explosions and the ashy coils of snake pellets. Lady Fingers and Black Cats fired off around us, and music blared from lawns and car radios. Eventually we arrived at the dam.

Its sides were already crowded, and we had to search for an open spot.

Once situated, we had a long wait until darkness. We listened to piped-in patriotic music and looked around for friends and neighbors. This was before cell phones, and, usually, we couldn't find any people we knew. We were an island of Piphers in a sea of holiday revelers.

I lay on the blanket and looked at the sunset sky. The children played frisbee with other nearby kids or explored our area. But by dark, we settled in together on the blanket. We shared cookies and apples and waited for the show.

Sara was a blonde schoolgirl and a budding comic tending toward sarcasm. When I called something we did "mother-daughter bonding," she suggested a better term would be "mother-daughter bondage." She was also a world-class talker. For every hour of lived experience, Sara could process for an hour, or two.

Both children were on swim teams, but Zeke was a champion swimmer who, by high school, swam hours a day. He also took karate and was a pitcher on his baseball team. When he came home after a day of swimming and karate, he would be ravenous. I would have dinner ready and watch as he scarfed down plates of lasagna or home-made enchiladas. Zeke and Jim were both good at imitations and extremely funny. I lived with three comedians.

During those years, I taught at the university, worked as a therapist, cleaned, cooked, chauffeured, helped with homework, and attended the children's musical, athletic, and school events. I was busy every minute, and I loved it. I felt so safe and happy. Finally, I had a stable family life and an organized household. Jim was playing in several good bands. The children had friends. Everyone came home for dinner.

Even then, I knew that one definition of happiness was lying on a blanket watching fireworks with my family. Zeke and Jim would stretch out on the blanket and Sara and I would snuggle in between them. At last, the first burst of glory would fill the sky, and a cheer went up from the crowd.

Our family critiqued every firework. We each picked our favorite display of the year. A few bursts took our breath away, and we could hear thousands of people simultaneously expressing their sense of wonder. But we loved them all—the white falling stars, the green or red bursts, the multicolored waterfalls of light, and the orange hoops expanding out to infinity. My favorite color was blue, although that color was the least frequent. Whenever a blue display appeared, one of the children would say, "There's one for you, mom."

Looking back, I realize that whole era was one for me. I loved having children around. I liked the nighttime tuck-ins, the Dairy Queen nights, the board games, and school carnivals. I savored every birthday party, holiday meal, swim meet, and violin concert. I relished the snow days when we made snow ice cream, went sledding and ice-skating, and built snow forts. At night, with all of us in bed as it blizzarded outside, I felt a great sense of well-being.

Childhood is as ephemeral as a display of exploding lights in the sky. By now my children are in their forties. Neither lives in Lincoln, and both are busy with their own big lives. We stay in close touch, but it is a rare treat to have family members sleeping under my roof.

What I still have, though, is the memory of those years with my young children. It is an idealized memory, made sunnier by time. Of course, Jim and I had arguments, and the children didn't always get along with us or each other. We were what Zorba the Greek called "the whole catastrophe." However, the great gift of memory is we can choose to live in the resplendent moments.

I can still hear Sara playing Für Elise on piano or the Bach Double on violin. I can see Zeke pitching in a city park on a hot summer night or coming home from high school in his yellow and black athletic jacket, his hair still wet from swim practice. I can hear the crunch of the leaves under our feet as we hiked in the Rockies and remember our tent conversations about bears and mountain lions.

I am grateful to have a well-stocked memory bank. I call it up when I am lonely or discouraged. I savor these slices of the past. They supply me with flashing blue bursts across the cold, gray winter skies.

Butterscotch Light

I come from a long line of sunset admirers. My grandmother walked a mile from the homestead to the mailbox every night at sunset. After a day of hard work on a Dust Bowl ranch, she loved the peace of a big sky. My aunts Betty and Margaret were fans as well, and I always felt happy walking with them on country roads at day's end.

When I was an adult and went home to visit, my mother and I would also take long walks at sunset. We would climb the steep hill to the south and then turn west to traverse a four-mile square. That walk afforded us ample time to see the sky change colors and to hear the quieting of the birds.

We passed a little pond surrounded by cottonwoods, a pasture with horses, old farmsteads, and wind-worn barns. In late May, the wheat fields were an inland sea of burnished gold, and in September, the ditches were filled with sunflowers and blazing sumac. In the fall, the light was the color of butterscotch. By the time we turned north for our last mile, we could see the first stars.

When these walks began, I had just discovered my mother's 1935 high school yearbook, bound with string and constructed of cardboard now worn soft as velvet. I asked about every one of the twenty students in her senior class. Who were her best friends? Who was smart, a hard worker, or easy to like?

Mother could tell me. While she was shy and socially awkward, her observation skills were first class. She could remember the girl who always had to be right, the pigeon-toed boy who dreamed of being a basketball star, and the anxious young woman who married the first man who asked her out. She could tell me who ate corn soup all winter long and whose dad died in a hailstorm.

We talked about the books I was reading. My mother had no time to read, but she liked to explore the questions my reading inspired. I liked to read about people from other cultures. My mother told me that she had changed her opinions over the years about native people, African Americans, and Asians. She said, "I would welcome people of any race into my family."

My mother also liked to share ethical dilemmas with me. She knew I was interested in decisions about how to deal with domestic violence or end-of-life issues. We disagreed on the topic of end-of-life. My mother believed all of life was sacred, and she opposed assisted suicide or euthanasia. I told her I could imagine a time when I would welcome medical help with dying.

For thirty years, whenever I returned to my hometown, my mother and I walked that four-mile square. She wore the same kind of sandals on every walk. They were made of strong cloth, open-toed and low-heeled. In the winter she wore them with socks. After wearing high heels for years, she had ruined her feet. Only these shoes made our walks possible.

Nothing gave my mother more pleasure than those outings. We walked through my college and graduate school years, my dad's strokes and death, my children's childhoods, and my years teaching and doing therapy. We walked until 1991. That year, one night about a mile into our walk, Mother said, "I need to sit down and rest."

She had never said that before. It was as if the axis of the earth had shifted. She was only seventy-three and looked as healthy and strong as the nearby horses. She still worked long days and slept only a few hours at night. A part of me had always thought my mother was eternal, like God or a mountain. By her words and actions, she had led us to believe that.

I looked at her as she sat on a big rock by the road. Her face was flushed and her breathing rapid. Watching her, I knew that she would be leaving me again and sooner than I had expected.

I felt a chunk of ice slowly move through my body and exit at my toes. This coldest of cold left me chilled for a long time after. Winter seemed already upon us.

Daughter Light

The year after I married Jim, Sara was born. She was a long, bony baby with eyes the color of black olives. As soon as she could communicate, she was pointing at clouds, animals, and people and asking, "Dat?" Then, "Dat?" She wanted to know the words, she wanted to know everything.

As a young girl, Sara was a kaleidoscope of color, emotion, and energy, always moving into new bright and sparkly patterns. She liked to dress in bright reds, purples, and greens, like a parrot.

When Sara heard a pinball machine, she asked, "What is that gleema, gleema sound?" When she heard a train, she echoed, "Clinka, clinka."

I can picture her at two, blonde and tan in a yellow sundress, eating a snow cone. At three, she is in a hot pink two-piece swimsuit, diving over and over in the shallow end of a public pool. At six, she stands onstage at our historic blues bar, the Zoo Bar, playing Bach's Minuet Two and Perpetual Motion with her quarter-size violin. When the crowd clapped and shouted approval, she appeared to be blown back by the force of the applause.

At Christmas, Sara and I snuggled in front of our fireplace in our matching pink-striped flannel pajamas. We made galaxy cookies, little wads of dough wrapped around chocolate chips, walnuts, or maraschino cherries, then baked, frosted, and topped with sparkles.

One day, when driving Sara to school, I hit a squirrel. Sara turned just in time to see it flopping around and bleeding on the street behind us. She sobbed so long and hard that she was coughing and choking. We returned home, and I canceled my appointments with my therapy clients. Sara was inconsolable until I told her we would join animal rescue.

Just as I was as a girl, Sara was always on a search to save animals. She lifted worms and caterpillars off sidewalks so they wouldn't be crushed by walkers or bikers. She insisted we stop for every turtle on the highway. We carried them off the road and out of danger.

The Christmas when Sara was six, she begged for a kitten. Jim and I were adamantly opposed. Sara suffered from mild asthma and had recently been ill with pneumonia. But, as was often the case with Sara, she launched argument after argument until we bowed to her will or, as Jim put it, "caved."

On Christmas Eve, we suggested Sara go look on her pink canopy bed. Zeke, Jim, and I all followed her into the bedroom to watch her discover the Siamese kitten curled up on her pillow. Sara gasped and, for a moment, just stared at the kitten in astonished silence. Eventually, she picked her up as if she were a sacred object or valuable piece of art. She cupped the kitty to her chest and talked gently to her. Sara's eyes were filled with a tenderness I can only imagine on the face of God.

Sara's motto could have been "It all looks good to me." As a schoolgirl, she took classes in poetry, art, and pottery. She liked spelling bees and field trips, swimming and outings to the Children's Zoo and Elephant Hall, our state's natural history museum.

While I cooked dinner, Sara would be nearby in our chilly north room, practicing Clementi's Sonatina in C Major or another song from the Suzuki repertoire. Every year, we attended all the musicals at our performing arts center and the university theater's production of *The Christmas Carol*, and Sara squeezed my hand as the curtains went up.

Most of all, she liked travel. When we were on vacation, Sara never wanted to come home. As we approached Lincoln from Yellowstone, Colorado, or the Ozarks, she would beg, "Let's just keep driving."

As an adult, Sara will sometimes ask me to bring her coffee. I will fill her cup as I would fill mine, and she will ask me to pour more. I will keep doing this until the coffee is just overflowing the cup. Then I will stop and say, "Sara, this is going to overflow."

Sara will respond, "That's just the way I like it. Overflowing."

Of course, like most mothers and daughters, we have had our struggles. Sara had an operatic emotional range, and her intense moods could be wearing. As a teenager, she would come toward me, then push me away. She often got angry at me for an unspoken thought. I would protest, and she would say, "I know what you were thinking."

And she would be right.

Sara's sensitivity to the world both predisposed her to sorrow and made her empathic and generous. By age thirteen, she was a vegetarian and member of PETA. She also worked with me at a place that offered homeless people coffee and a shower.

My mother told me that when old men were dying, they often hallucinated that they were driving home though a blizzard. They would call out to their team of horses, "Keep on. Keep on. I see a light in the window." She said that when old women were dying, they called out for their mothers. Perhaps when we are dying, we will call out for our daughters as well.

Through all my years with Sara, in spite of our stormy times and her current faraway life in Canada, we have always kept close tabs on each other's day-to-day lives and relational and emotional experiences. We understand each other at the deepest possible level.

There is a thread of light that runs through our relationship. And that moon-silver thread loops back in time to my own mother and my Grandmother Page, to my Scottish great-grandmother and beyond to our first mother, the mother of us all.

My Mother's Death

The last year of her life, Mother was in the hospital. She suffered from multiple health issues including diabetes and kidney failure, and she had had heart attacks and cancer. I lived three hours away, but I was her family support system. At the time, Jim played gigs every weekend night, and Sara was a teenager in need of supervision. I was working full-time as a therapist and a supervisor of graduate students' clinical practicums. I needed triplicate copies of myself. Still, I made it to Kansas at least once a week and, toward the end, sometimes twice a week.

Meanwhile, like most people who suffer long hospital stays, my mother grew weaker and less alert. Eventually, my lively and sharp mother was in a wheelchair and unable to name the current president. When I visited, I would bring a book, a La Croix for myself, and black coffee for her. Sometimes she would ask for something special to eat. Once, it was liverwurst. Another time, fresh green grapes.

Mother was stoic to a fault. One day when the nurse asked her how she was feeling, she said, "Good. I am not as nauseous as I was yesterday."

The nurse looked surprised and I asked, "Mom, did you tell anyone you were nauseous yesterday?"

"No," she said, "I didn't think it important."

When I asked about her health, she would often reply, "Let's talk about something more interesting."

She was eager for stories about my family. I spared her all but the happy ones. She liked to hear Jim's latest corny jokes and band stories. She wanted to know about my writing courses. She had high hopes that I would someday be published.

The present was dreadful, but we enjoyed our past. We talked about the Ozark summers, memorable restaurant meals, and my children when they were babie.

I reminded her of the time we forgot Pixie Rosarita at a muddy lake in Kansas. When we went back to look for her, she was waiting patiently where we had parked our car. Mother liked to hear me reminisce about the beaches on the Gulf Coast and the family reunions where she and her sisters stayed up past midnight drinking coffee and eating pie.

Mother was skilled at denial and didn't plan to die. She held on through one crisis after another and submitted to ever more restrictive and invasive procedures just to stay alive. She didn't sign a Do Not Resuscitate order, and she assured me she would soon be well enough to go home.

She often experienced hallucinations. One was of making spaghetti and meatballs. She would say, "Hurry up now with those onions." Or, "I need more tomatoes and oregano." In another she was delivering babies. "Steady now, push, push." Or, "Nurse, make sure you catch that baby. Hold on tight."

By the end she could barely move or speak. She lay in an ICU full of tubes.

The last time I visited, Mother was almost gone, but she could see and hear me. I made up a bedtime story that took place during the Korean War when my father was away. I told her that the sounds we were hearing were the gurgles of a mountain stream. I described our picnic of sandwiches and deviled eggs and how we took off our shoes, rolled up our pants, and splashed in the ice-cold, fast-moving water. High above us the sky was royal blue. Mountain blue we called it.

The air was crisp and smelled like the pines. I told her that the lights on the ICU machines were the lights of Denver, far in the distance. We could only see a few now, but as the sun dropped behind the Rockies and we drove down the mountains into the city, the lights would be brighter. When we reached the lights, we would be almost home.

Like her father, my mother never wanted to be alone. However, she died alone.

I was between therapy clients when a nurse called to tell me that Mother had died. When I heard the news, I didn't feel sad, I felt gone. Numb. Entirely cut off from my emotions.

After Mother's death, those same chunks of ice rolled through my body. I shivered even in my thick sweaters, and, at night, I needed extra blankets. We are never too old to be orphaned.

I am not sure yet that I have accepted my mother's loss. I still have moments when I want to call her and tell her something. When I see one of my grandchildren doing something beautiful, I wish she could see it. When I eat in a magnificent restaurant, I wish she could taste the food. My mother comes to me at night in my dreams, and I am so happy to see her. I hear her voice in my head every day. She says, "Be kind to each other."

Writing

After I started work as a psychologist and had children, I had a few years when I had trouble finding the time to take a shower or call a close friend. But when Sara was in third grade, I began to have small windows of discretionary time. I thought carefully about how I would like to use these precious moments of time to myself. One morning I experienced a revelation: "I want to write. I have wanted that all of my life and now I am going to do it. I don't even care if I'm not good at it or if no one ever sees it. I'm going to respect my own need to put words on paper."

At first, I journaled. I wrote all of the things I could not say—my worries about my children, my irritations with Jim, and my fears about a nuclear war or climate change. I also recorded the many things in my life that were good. I loved my work, my family, and all my friends. I was dancing to live music almost every weekend and reading big books after the children went to bed. I knew how lucky I was.

I wrote about my mother's death. By the time she died, she was so diminished that a part of me was grateful that she could let go. But when that small, diminished, suffering woman died, so did my brilliant, hardworking, storytelling mother.

I was no longer numb with the pain of my mother's death. Instead, as I wrote, I often cried.

I approached writing as I approached much of learning, by reading about it and going to classes. I ordered and read dozens of books on writing and attended workshops within a two-hundred-mile radius of Lincoln. I joined the Nebraska Wesleyan writers' group.

Twyla was a poet in one of my classes. Over coffee one day, she and I decided to form a writers' group, and we invited three other women into it. We named it the Prairie Trout, and we have been writing together for thirty-five years.

At first, I woke at five in the morning and wrote at the kitchen table until it was time to wake up the children and make their breakfast. Before they came to the kitchen, I cleared the table of my writing. We had some scrambled eggs and muffins, and we all left for work or school.

After about a year of this, I decided I needed an office of my own. We had a "guest room" in the basement that was really just a dark room with a bed in it and some things we were storing. I bought myself a small desk, tidied up the room, and declared my office off-limits.

Having a room of my own made a tremendous difference. I first wrote letters to the editor and then editorials. I also began writing short essays that I read on our public radio station once a week. After a couple of fiction classes, I wrote a few short stories. One of them won a prize, but I decided fiction wasn't for me. There were so many talented fiction writers. I needed to find a form of writing that I could do better than most people. In other words, I wanted to discover what I alone could say.

At my office, I was seeing many women with eating disorders. This was a new phenomenon all over America. There had always been a few women with anorexia, but our country was experiencing an epidemic. We had no conceptual framework or treatment protocols. We didn't even have language. Many of the women I saw didn't know how to describe their problems.

Because of my heavy caseload with these women, I developed my own ways of helping them. I looked at the problem from a feminist cultural perspective instead of from an individual pathology perspective. I devised some methods for treatment that involved becoming a cultural observer, especially of women's magazines, women in media, and our general obsession with thinness.

Because no one was writing anything about treatment at that time, I self-published a book on my ways of helping women. I called this book *Hunger Pains.* A friend designed its cover and another friend edited and printed it.

Soon I was driving around Nebraska with a case of books in the trunk of my car. I was giving workshops on eating disorders to therapists, nurses, and schoolteachers. *Hunger Pains* went through several printings. I started thinking about writing another book. Maybe this time I would find a publisher.

My next book was called *Reviving Ophelia* and was about my teenage clients. After it was published in 1994, I began my career as a professional writer.

The great gift I gave myself was listening to my own voice. For one of the first times in my life, I was able to quiet the voices of others and do what I most wanted to do.

Writing brought a new kind of light into my life. It was the light of living life twice, once in real time and once in reflective time. It allowed me to grow into my true self. Writing gave me an intellectually challenging life in which I could still live quietly in my own home.

As a writer, I can do the things I loved to do when I was a girl. Almost every day, I read, I swim, I spend time outdoors and with my friends. I still spend my time telling stories.

I found my life's calling in therapy and in writing. Both activities require every ounce of my intelligence and every aspect of my personality. Both allow me to learn what I alone can contribute to the universe. We are fortunate if we can find work that illuminates our lives and warms our hearts.

Fame

When *Reviving Ophelia* rocketed to number one on the *New York Times* bestseller list, I was not prepared. I had expected that my main reward for writing this book would be learning to write with a New York editor. Instead, I was catapulted into a spotlight, something I had never wanted. The first effect of this spotlight was that people began to treat me differently. Even my extended family teased me about being famous. Some people in our community who had never spoken to me invited me to dinner. People on the street recognized me, but I didn't recognize them. I felt bad that I might be hurting their feelings. When I went to parties or events, I pushed myself to speak to everyone so that no one would think that I was snobby. All this effort to reassure people I liked them wore me out.

Like many midwestern women, I had been taught never to stand out or consider myself special. Besides, I knew I wasn't the best writer, even in my own writing group. I had just written some new ideas based on my experiences as a therapist.

I was bombarded by requests to speak, to consult, to do interviews, to co-write books, and to sign book deals. I was asked to do everything from being on corporate boards to giving product endorsements and to helping distraught parents of adolescent girls find a therapist. I didn't have enough hours in the day to respond to all these requests.

Jim took over almost all the responsibilities for answering the phone and dealing with requests. This soon became an eight-hour workday for him. He was a kind therapist who spent many hours a day as a free referral service. This was before email and the internet and everything was done with paper or telephones.

I was still working as a therapist, and now I was writing a new book. I also had speeches to prepare. I woke at four in the morning to try to keep up with this schedule.

After dinner, Jim and I would take a walk and discuss the difficult issues that had come up that day. We devised policies that helped us make decisions quickly. I wouldn't do product endorsements or be on corporate boards. I didn't want to co-write books or consult. But I would do interviews and help promote my books.

On the road making speeches, I was green as grass. At first, I traveled alone, flying mostly to the East and West

Coasts. The people I met were pleasant, but I was continually stressed. I worried about missing flights and the responsibility of earning the money I was being paid. I wondered if I would have the energy to be kind and attentive to the hundreds of strangers who would want a word with me.

Meanwhile, I had trouble meeting my own basic needs. I could not sleep in new settings. Some of the places I spent the night made me crazy. For example, at a private girl's school in the Northeast, I was lodged in a museum, and the doors were locked at night. It was a roomy, dark, old building with an ancient bedroom for me. But I hadn't had any dinner, I couldn't get out of the place, and there was no way for me to use a telephone, as the switchboard operator had gone home. Another time, my bedroom was in an administration building, and, at two in the morning, the cleaning crew came in and vacuumed around my bed. I never returned to sleep.

At one point, I did a two-day workshop for professionals in Illinois. Knowing I would be in front of large crowds of psychologists, I was unable to sleep at all during the two nights I worked there. By the end of the second day, I couldn't hold my thoughts together. I was in front of five hundred people and forgetting the beginning of my sentence before I reached the end.

One year I slept more in hotel rooms than in my own bed. As my public persona grew, my real self became smaller and more fragile. I discovered I was a person who only did well around familiar people in my own territory. I needed that grounding to stay calm and to sleep at night.

This all came to a head at a November gig in 2002 in Defiance, Ohio. Jim and I flew on three different planes through snow to an airport a couple of hours from the small college where I was speaking. Two of the planes had experienced engine trouble, and by the time we reached the airport, both of us were exhausted from the stress of the flights. We were also hungry, and I was giving a speech that night. But we were driving through a desolate landscape of mostly industrial parks and empty fields.

Finally, we stopped at a small-town café. There were dead flies around the inside windows and dust on some of the tables, but we had no alternative. I needed to eat before I spoke. I had been reading *Fast Food Nation* on the plane and was even more concerned than usual that my food be healthy. Jim and I ordered bowls of chili. When this chili came and I tasted it, I thought it tasted like actual shit.

I didn't finish the bowl, and I told Jim that either we were in a place where we were eating fecal matter for dinner or I was so messed up that I was imagining I was eating fecal matter. "Either way," I said, "I need to get off the road."

That winter I stayed home. I lay on the couch by my fire with my little cat on my lap and read big history books. I didn't have the energy to see my friends. My blood pressure was high and I started on medication. I also began reading about Buddhism and meditating.

By spring, I was doing some speaking again, but with a greatly curtailed schedule.

From these experiences, I learned that nothing was glamorous. Glamor was in the eye of the beholder, not the person performing or working in the spotlight. Expensive hotel rooms and bouquets of flowers were no substitute for watching the stars blink on and the sun and moon rise. Kind people in book lines did not keep me from missing my friends. To feel truly alive, I needed the sights, sounds, and smells of home.

Okinawa

In 1995, I was invited to work in Okinawa. This was just after the armed services had resolved to fully integrate women into their ranks. The navy needed gender education, and I was selected to be a speaker.

The military gives people a rank so that it knows where to put them in the hierarchy. I can't remember my rank, but it was high, and Jim and I were given the generals' guesthouse. This was a spacious four-room apartment with leather-bound books, a fully stocked bar, and elegant furniture.

During my time on this island, almost everything I saw reminded me of my father. Fifty years earlier, my father had been here as a navy medic with the invading force whose mission was to dislodge the Japanese troops.

In the mid-1940s, Okinawa had been a steamy place with almost impenetrable jungles. The only way to move forward was to hack through the roots and vines, always alert for landmines, ambushes, and poisonous snakes, most colored the green of the vegetation.

The Japanese had burrowed into caves underground and were determined to hold on even if it meant the death of all. The battle for territory was fought foot by foot, with many Americans dying from surprise attacks, aerial bombardment, and hand-to-hand combat. Through it all, my father ran from man to man with a stretcher and an emergency medical kit. He didn't carry a gun, and the Japanese troops did not spare the medics.

Dad picked up men with faces torn off or limbs shattered, dodging bullets as he hauled the injured to medical tents. He must have seen a thousand deaths or more, including those of many friends. He witnessed people stabbing each other with bayonets, and men who had been blown apart.

At the same time, he was not living in the generals' quarters. He was a grunt, sleeping in a tent on the sand or in a small clearing in the jungle. He was covered in insect bites, always hot, and unable to shower or relax.

When he wrote his mother, he never mentioned the death, the trauma, or the constant risk of being wounded or killed. Instead, he wrote, "The food is terrible, but fortunately the water is even worse."

Jim and I dined in the officers' mess, where we were offered fine wine and fresh-caught fish. We were given tours of the island. Under a light-blue sky, dark waves rolled onto white sand. Ribbons of orchids cascaded down the sides of waterfalls. The hills were covered with stone graves that looked like turtle shells. During the battle for Okinawa, two hundred thousand people died, including one quarter of the Okinawan civilians.

We visited a center by the sea that Pearl S. Buck had funded to promote American-Asian friendship after the war. Now a silver-haired American octogenarian dressed in a kimono was in charge. She offered us tea and then took us to see the nearby cliffs. Pointing to the sharp rocks far below, she said that when the Americans arrived, this was where many Okinawans jumped to their deaths. The Japanese had told them that Americans were monsters who would torture and kill them all. As I stood by this serene woman in this peaceful place, I could hardly take in all of the suffering that had happened here.

Our last gift from the military was a cottage on a private beach where officers took their vacations. We snorkeled in the East China Sea and walked through the orchid-filled gardens. At night, Jim and I sat on the beach and watched the sun set over what was for us a new ocean. When the stars emerged, the few constellations that we recognized were upside down. We focused on Canopus, the great star of the south, and on Sirius, the Dog Star we knew from home.

My father was in his early twenties when he signed up for the war. At that age, I was in college. During the war, he had been self-sacrificing and courageous, yet he never shared a feast with officers, stayed in a beach house, or snorkeled with a hundred kinds of colorful fish.

Now his daughter, through many strokes of good fortune, was here too. We each had our destinies. His life was short and filled with events I can hardly imagine. Fate had been much kinder to me.

Luck is not evenly distributed. There is not always a connection between effort and reward. Some heroes go unsung. My father's willingness to give his young life, to run through bullets and jungle to rescue others, is one definition of heroic.

Every night on that beach seven thousand miles away from his home and mine, I thought of my father. He had been so angry at my brothers and me for opposing the Vietnam War. Our marching against the war must have felt like a betrayal. He had been willing to fight for his country. He had sacrificed so much and been scarred emotionally by war. Then his own children sang Pete Seeger's "Study War No More."

My father did the best he could, just as we all do. One definition of adulthood is that we can see our parents as people, independent of their relationships with us. Looking at the night sky, I could see Frank Bray, not as my father, but as a person who, like all of us, was caught in the tides of his times.

Teardrops in the Snow

When my grandsons Coltrane and Otis were eight and four, Sara and John moved the family to Canada. John had been offered a good job near Toronto, and he and Sara were ready for an adventure. Both had lived most of their lives in Nebraska, and they looked forward to a new country and a more cosmopolitan environment.

The boys had been born in Lincoln, and we had been with them nearly every day. They had brought so much light and lightheartedness into our lives. We couldn't imagine life without that family twenty blocks away. When I heard they were leaving, I had chest pains that sent me to a cardiologist I am still seeing.

Otis was too young to understand what moving meant, but Coltrane didn't want to leave. He loved his school, his house, his cousins, and his friends. He was close to Jim and me and accustomed to spending lots of time at our home. He wrote an essay to his parents pleading with them to stay in Lincoln. In the weeks before their journey, Coltrane hugged me fiercely at every parting.

While his parents readied for the move, Jim and I watched the boys more than usual. We had a cold snowy winter, and we spent time making snowmen and sledding on Holmes Dam. Coltrane and Jim played lots of ping-pong. They had so many inside jokes that Coltrane often fell on the floor laughing.

I drove the children to the library where we picked out big stacks of books. Otis and I would cuddle up in a recliner, and I would read him *Mother Goose* or *Curious George*.

The boys often stayed overnight. Jim and I would take turns rocking Otis. Coltrane and I talked or read side by side far into the night. It was a sacred time, made all the more beautiful by the knowledge it would end soon.

This separation from close family was as hard on me as the one I had experienced with my mother when I was a young girl. I wasn't sure I could, or even wanted to, live through it. In the night, I would wake with my chest tight and my mood as black as a starless sky.

In February, we celebrated Otis's birthday with an orange truck cake. Orange was his favorite color, and as much as possible, he wore orange shoes, coats, and shirts. Driving around town we pointed out every orange vehicle. Now, years after Otis's move, I still feel the urge to point out orange trucks and cars.

Everything was poignant during the week before Sara's family left. Filling a sippy cup, putting on Otis's snow boots, or watching Coltrane make origami cranes—all of it beautiful, but right on the edge of heartbreak.

The night before their journey north, the family stayed at our place. We ordered Indian takeout and had one last evening of Uno and bedtime stories. Jim and I stayed with the boys until they fell asleep.

In the morning, after a quick breakfast, we walked out into the snow to say goodbye. We hugged everyone tightly. Coltrane and I found it hard to let go of each other, but we had no choice. Then it was happening. Sara checked the children's seat belts and closed the car doors. We stood in the driveway waving as their family drove out of sight.

I didn't cry. In fact, I didn't feel anything. I went numb, the way I had in Missouri when I was six and, much later, when my mother died. I didn't feel grief as much as I felt dead. When I experience loss, the lights go out.

Jim wrote a song about that parting called "Teardrops in the Snow."

John told us later that, as he had watched the two of us grow smaller in his rearview mirror, he cried and cried. He realized for the first time what this separation meant for us.

I still yearn for that family. I had hoped to be at every soccer game, school program, and swim party. I had wanted to be with those boys until they grew up or I died. However, it was not to be.

Sara and John have done a good job staying in touch. Sara calls often and sends pictures and videos. John sets up FaceTimes and happy hours. We talk to the boys on Sunday morning and sometimes in between.

In 2019, we traveled to Canada every two or three months, and we were there to celebrate Coltrane's October birthday and Otis's in February. We were together at Christmas and for three weeks in the summer.

Sara and John are happy in their Canadian town. They have work they enjoy and friends from all over the world. The grandsons like their schools. Otis is learning to speak French. I don't begrudge them their choices. As an adult, I didn't make major life decisions to please my mother. That is not the American way.

Yet, in my bones I feel that we hominids were designed to be with family. We thrived because we were tribal. Grandparents helped raise grandchildren and children took care of the old relatives when the time came.

I know our world is no longer arranged that way, but I must say I wish it were.

When Zeke's son was four, he said to me, "I wish we could build a house right by yours and have a little hall from my bedroom right into your living room."

I told him I wished for the same thing.

Equatorial Light

On June 2019, our family of eleven was at a beautiful cabin called Casa de Dorado on Playa Grande in Costa Rica. Sara's family had flown in from Toronto for the first family reunion since they had moved away. The yard was filled with flowers, and there were parrots and monkeys in the trees. The sky was blue and the turquoise sea sparkled in the constant sunlight. The equatorial light was new to us, bright and flat, with sunrise and sunset near six A.M. and six P.M. every day.

We were near Tamarindo, with some of the best surfing in the world. However, the beaches were known for their riptides and drownings. Still, we were in the water every day. Zeke taught his kids to surf, and he surfed when he wasn't fishing. Sara and John watched their kids play closer to shore. Two days before our departure we were out bobbing in the waves and body surfing.

Sara, my daughter-in-law Jamie and I swam beyond the white water to ride the swells. We could almost float in the salty water, and we lost track of time as we drifted up and down on the waves. After a while, Jamie said quietly, "This feels rip-tidey."

I wasn't experiencing that, but mindful of all the warnings, I said immediately, "Let's go in."

It was then I noticed we were way beyond the breakers. The figures on shore were the size of tooth-picks, the white-capped waves seemed miles away, almost beyond reach. I had never before been so far out in the sea.

Meanwhile, I felt a strong undertow. I wasn't sure if it was a riptide or simply a strong tide going out. My upper body and lower body were being pulled in different directions. When I swam directly toward shore, I could make no progress. Next, I swam parallel to the shore, then turned in but, when I looked up, I was the same distance from the beach.

I was tired and scared. I recalled all the warnings about drownings by the State Department, guidebooks, and friends. My friend Gretchen's family had almost been washed out to sea by a rogue wave. I thought, *this could be it for me.* This didn't make me sad. I had never been afraid of death; I had been afraid of loss. Surprisingly, I felt calm and logical. I thought, *I hope Jamie and Sara are okay. I can't see them and I am not strong enough to save them.*

When I looked to shore, I was relieved to see Zeke was watching us. He was a strong swimmer and a lifeguard. I struggled on, aware I was not moving forward. I thought, what a strange way to end my life. This will ruin our beautiful vacation. And, if the three of us drown, our families will be so traumatized. And Sara and I won't finish the book project we were working on together. And I will miss all of Jim's summer band jobs. It was a muddle of thoughts, but I felt surprisingly unemotional. Almost philosophical and abstract.

Meanwhile, I was exhausted and at least as far out to sea as when I started trying to swim in. I flipped over on my back and let the waves carry me while I caught my breath. I hoped that if I could just stay afloat, Zeke would eventually find me.

After a while, I heard the sound of waves breaking. Soon after I felt the spray of white water. I realized, I am going in. I am going on.

When I reached the beach, I lay in the sand and looked for Sara and Jamie. Both were almost to shore. The noonday light was almost the color of the white sand. Around me, tourists played and talked as if nothing had happened.

I was so tired that I couldn't stand up. My family came over. Zeke gave me water and almonds. Eventually, I rose from the sand and walked to our cabin to fix lunch. What had saved me was stopping the struggle.

Chinook Salmon

The first September we visited Sara's family in Canada, we hiked by waterfalls and played soccer in their city park. This park was at the base of a mountain flaming rose-red with maples. The komorebi of sparkling, almost pink light shining through the maple leaves knocked me out.

I had had a lifetime goal of seeing Chinook salmon spawning, and in Sara's small town it was happening. We reached them by parking at a grocery store and crossing a bridge on a busy street. That didn't seem like an aesthetically pleasing way to view salmon, but when we hiked down to the creek, the nearby town no longer mattered. We were with the salmon.

Twenty fish formed a spawning nest. They were grouped in twos or threes with the occasional lone fish. Chinook can be five feet long and weigh up to 120 pounds. The ones we witnessed were smaller, but not by much. They had hooked jaws and were no longer the blue-silver fish they had been in the ocean. They were darker, and some had a red or green hue.

After spending up to eight years in the ocean, they had returned to the exact place they were born. They were old now and would die soon, but they moved relentlessly against the strong current in the clear, cold creek. They faced a steep waterfall but, like all salmon, they carried a centuries-old determination to return to their natal stream. Their inborn devotion to the next generation would cost them their lives.

As these dying salmon moved in the sparkling water, I fell into deep time. My life became connected to the lives of these beautiful fish. My heart softened and expanded as I experienced the interconnections we share with all living species. This ancient kinship is the deepest connection I can feel.

The Fabtones' Last Night
at the Zoo Bar

On New Year's Eve 1999, my husband's band played for all their friends at an event space called the Loft. That night everyone filled the dance floor. We were middle-aged, in the midst of busy lives, and relatively untouched by fears for the future. We boogied to "Good Rockin' Daddy," "Wild Nights," and "Pretty Woman." We embraced one another and formed conga lines around the room. By then, the Fabtones had been together for fifteen years, and they had built a community of friends and fans. At midnight we toasted the new millennium with champagne.

New Year's Eve 2019, the Fabtones hosted another gathering for 140 of their friends. But this time, the party was to say farewell. The crowd was mostly the same people, but we had greatly changed. Our hair was gray or silver, our faces had wrinkles and lines, and we weren't as spry as we had been. Many of us had retired, and our children had grown up and moved on to their adult lives. Nowadays we visited doctors' offices more often than we danced.

I boogied with Twyla, who had lost her husband the year before, and with Jill, whom I had known for forty-five years. When I met Jill, she was a pretty, vibrant student nurse dating Reynold, the drummer in a band with Jim. Jill was still pretty, but she had retired from nursing, and she and Reynold owned a lake cabin.

Wallace Stegner wrote, "We thought we were going to make our mark on the world and instead, the world made marks on us." Most of us were pretty marked up. Lora, the vibrant owner of a local bookstore, had multiple sclerosis, and Sam had late-stage Parkinson's. Roger, John, and Tom had died. Frank and Quinn had lost their life partners. Eric's wife of thirty years left him last Christmas, and he hadn't spoken to his sons since then. Donna's son was in alcohol treatment.

However, most of us were content. Our children, if we had them, were well launched. Some of us were lucky enough to be grandparents.

Almost all of us were still dancing with the people who brought us to the party. Walt and Kay were in a bluegrass band, and Cora had taken up watercolor. Ray was playing music and enjoying a new job teaching. And we were at a party with champagne, neon lights over the bar, and a great dance band.

Sally, in her wheelchair, waved her arms and twisted her body to the music. I danced to "The Monkey Time," "Chain of Fools," and "Giving It Up for Your Love." I was moving among my friends for joy and to fend off my grief that the thirty-five-year-old era of the Fabtones was ending. I would never hear the band play these songs again, and most likely, I would never again be in a room dancing with this big group of friends.

Onstage the band was pulling out all the stops. Jon's sax solos were ornate and showy, and when he stepped to the front of the stage, his instrument lit up with Christmas lights. Reynold knocked us out when he sang "Domino" and "Brown Eyed Girl." No one but Van Morrison could match him. Pam belted out a raucous version of "Empty Bed Blues" and poured her heart into "(Sittin' On) The Dock of the Bay" and "Crazy." Steve played his virtuoso guitar. Jim backed it all up with his steady bass. Such wonderful music. How could they let this end?

But the musicians weren't ending this era, time was. After multiple health problems, Jon felt he could no longer handle the practice required to keep up his chops. Steve now vacationed in Florida three months a year. The dance clubs, which had been the bread and butter of this band's circuit, were closing down. The Fabtones' time was up.

All evening I felt a mixture of joy and sorrow. I loved dancing and singing along to old favorites such as "Doctor My Eyes" and "The Letter." However, I was witnessing the end of an era in a wild and wise community. I would see most of my friends again, but not at a dance party.

My children were middle-aged now, and my oldest granddaughter was in college. My hands didn't work well, my eyes weren't good, and I could no longer carry a pack up a mountain. But I was happy, and the people on the dance floor and stage had played a large role in that. All these many years, we had been as intertwined as prairie grasses, living together for the new green spring, scorching summers, brightly colored autumns, and snowy winters. We had faced all kinds of weather together. And we no doubt would face more.

However, this night we swirled to "Moondance" and "Mercy Mercy Me." We stretched it out with "Memphis in the Meantime." We shouted "I love you" to one another across the crowded dance floor. The banded ended the night with Guy Clark's "Old Friends."

We all sang along on the chorus.

We lifted our champagne glasses for one last toast. We hugged each other. Then, the neon lights blinked on and off. It was closing time. We walked into the dark and cold of New Year's 2020. We had no idea of the harsh weather we would soon face.

Snowfields

On a Saturday afternoon I drove into the rolling
hills of Nebraska's Bohemian Alps en route to my
annual retreat with my Jamie. The first weekend every
January, we indulge ourselves in thirty-six hours of
freedom from our responsibilities. We bring hiking
boots, journals, candles, books, and wine. We walk in
the hills and talk about the years behind and ahead of us.

We have seen each other during the year, but never
without family. Here we are friends, listening closely so
that we can understand each other's experience. We have
the time and space to be reflective.

When Jamie was first dating Zeke, we had a chance
encounter. On the loading dock of the Mill, a coffeehouse downtown, I was reading Turgenev's *Fathers and
Sons* when Jamie rode up on her bike. She was a college
student, tall with long, dark hair and beautiful in a

Katharine Hepburn way. Jamie waved to me as she locked her bike. Then she pulled *The Brothers Karamazov* out of her backpack. I thought to myself, *We are going to get along just fine.*

Now, twenty years later, I am on my way to once again read books with Jamie. As I drive, I listen to the music of Kitka, an eastern European women's choir. This ancient music, the snowy rural landscape, and the afternoon winter sky give me a peaceful feeling.

The Bohemian Alps is a beautiful area of rolling hills, deep valleys, and little creeks. Scrub cedars are scattered across the white shoulders of the land. In some places, the snow flashes silver from the sunlight.

On this route, I always think of my mother. Dorchester is on the southern tip of the area, and when we lived there, we ate like the Czechs. I liked jaternice, kolaches, liver dumplings, and roasted goose with sauerkraut. Most of my mother's patients were Bohemians. She described them as working hard and playing hard, with a strong love of family and a sense of the tragic and poetic. After years of living in a town with Czechs, I agree with my mother.

I drove past red and green combines, silver silos, and Angus cattle. I watched for a particular gray hay shed curving toward a fall. It had so many wooden slats missing that it was see-through. Every year I wondered if it would be gone, but this year it was still standing and only slightly more hunched than it had been the year before.

My eyes searched out the faded old barns, the little creeks, and the lone cottonwoods standing in fallow fields. After weeks in the city, these sunlight-on-snow views were like medicine to me—potions from a forgotten time, a quieter, emptier time, when I was young and the world felt younger too.

A red-tailed hawk sat on a fence post, and Canada geese circled a small pond and set their wings for the drop down. Just outside Loma, I watched a stack of gulls spiraling, then spreading across the silvering sky.

As I approached St. Benedict Center, the egg yolk sun touched the horizon and long blue shadows striped the snow ivory. As I crossed Bone Creek and the ice-jammed Platte, I fell into a state of grace. Kitka, the land, the birds, and even the faded tractors along a shelterbelt all became sacralized. I wondered as I always do—how is it that grace descends upon us? We can't will it or manufacture it ourselves. Rather, it comes to us in the same way as a murmuration of starlings and as random as falling stars.

I check into the center and walk through the brick and timbered halls garlanded with greens. I pass the solarium, my favorite room, with its fireplace, book-shelves, and floor-to-ceiling windows.

In a nearby meeting room I can hear Los Pescadoros laughing and talking. These are people from Central

America and the Yucatan, mostly Mayans, who work in the meatpacking plants. Every year, they come the same time that Jamie and I do. They bring snacks, sodas, and energy. For many of the workers, this is their one vacation of the year. They sing and dance to the music of electric guitars, and they invite Jamie and me to join them.

Other evenings, we walk across the road to hear the Benedictine priests from all over the world sing Compline.

As I unpacked in my Spartan room, the white lights in the trees blinked on. I could see the last rays of sunset in the pink and orange surface of the lake.

I knocked on Jamie's door, and soon we were telling each other our most interesting news. I had traveled a great deal in 2019—every other month to Canada, to San Francisco to see my brother, to the Northwest for two weeks to celebrate our forty-fifth wedding anniversary, and to D.C. to participate in Reverend William Barber's Poor People's Campaign.

Many things had changed since we started these retreats. Jamie and Zeke's children had grown from toddlers into teenagers. Kate had graduated from high school and left for college. Jim had closed out an old band and started a new one. I had broken bones and lost hand strength. I once had carried fifty-pound children, and this last year I couldn't lift a farmer's market pumpkin.

I looked into the fire and saw the blue flames and the sparks of all those years. They floated and faded before me the same way that time does.

We talked of the year to come. As usual, I had travel plans to Canada, to work at Camp Denali, and to visit Scotland. Jamie had a trip planned with Zeke—a twentieth anniversary vacation to the beach. I wanted to host a seventieth birthday celebration for Jim.

For a few moments, we considered the virus in China that had just been discovered. We wondered if it would come to our country. Maybe, we agreed. But it was unlikely to affect us here in Nebraska or change our lives in any significant way.

St. Benedict's was filled with light. During the day, winter sunlight poured into the solarium. At night, the trees around the lake were festooned in white light. At that moment, my life seemed sun-filled too. As Jamie and I celebrated this time of joy together, we could not imagine the darkness that would soon descend on the world.

January Ice

In January 2020, my brothers and their partners flew into Lincoln for a four-day visit. Jake and Sally live in San Francisco and John and Becky are in North Carolina.

The last time my brothers and I were together was twenty years ago at my son's wedding. Since then, I had seen John and Jake separately, and my brothers had twice traveled together to Alaska. Now, finally, after twenty years, we managed to reunite in my big old house in Lincoln. We weren't skinny tow-headed kids anymore or even strong middle-aged adults. We all had gray hair and stooped shoulders. But some parts of us hadn't changed with time. We were readers and animal lovers, big talkers.

Even though we had always been close, we had frequently been separated. We carried many sad stories from the troubled family we grew up in. Unfortunately, the weight of these stories played a role in our lack of reunions. None of us liked to remember the bullying at school and abuse from our dad at home. As children, we were clumsy outsiders, and, when we could, we had all moved far from Nebraska. Only I returned.

By now, we had all lived big lives far from our childhoods. We had found loving partners and met our own kind. We had worked in professions we loved. Life had become easier for us. In 2020, happiness brought us together.

John and Becky arrived late Thursday afternoon. We talked as the sun set behind us, its showy colors glinting off the lake in the east. Later, we had potato soup and a loaf of dense, chocolaty rye bread that Becky had baked.

On Friday the weather was cold and the streets were icy. The airport closed before Jake's flight could arrive. Instead, he and Sally were routed through Omaha and Ubered to our house around midnight.

Waiting up for them, we felt like children at Christmas, excited for Santa. When Jake and Sally arrived, we laughed and talked our way into the early hours of the morning. We felt oddly exalted to be together.

Both of my brothers resembled big shaggy bears. Jake looked like my mother, and John looked like my father. They both appeared fierce and their voices were gruff, but I knew them to be as gentle as kittens. When they laughed, they both lowered their heads to their chests as if they were embarrassed by joy. Their chuckles sounded like a bear would sound if bears could laugh.

Because of the cold and the ice, we stayed in all weekend. Becky baked us an apple pie. We told jokes and traded book and movie reviews. We took turns cooking and entertaining each other. I explained the art of the free-write. Jake and Jim played guitars. Sally, a former ballerina, now a ballet teacher, gave us a lesson. Jake had been taking lessons, but John and I had never even stood in first position, let alone done a plié.

We watched the sunsets and sunrises. One morning Becky woke up first and saw a bald eagle, prey in its claws, do a flyby. That same night at sunset we saw a fox in our driveway.

Over the three days we talked about everything except our childhoods. We had never agreed about our parents' culpability. Even though I was aware of their many mistakes, I loved them. My brothers were less forgiving. Our father had died in 1974 and our mother in 1992. Decades later, we didn't choose to revisit that argument. We had outgrown it. We had better stories now.

We chose to live in one of those better stories, one about how close we were and how much we wanted to be together.

During that final meal together, John made a toast: "To the happiest four days of my life." Finally, after many years of separation, we had decided it was time to come home—to each other.

The next morning, when I woke at 6:30, my brother Jake joined me for coffee. He pulled his folding chair close to mine. I suggested he move to a more comfortable chair, and he said, "I want to sit by you."

When I remarked that he was up early, Jake said, "I was waiting for you to wake up."

Becky made us fresh raspberry scones. As people packed, I drank coffee with whoever had time for me. When we gathered just before parting, we decided to have another reunion the next year.

But who knew if there would be a next year? We were getting old and all of us had health problems. Knowledge of our finitude had helped us love one another even more. And we clumsy grown Bray children had just danced ballet together.

VII

Resilience

Helicopter Lights

R. W. Emerson wrote two centuries ago, "Events are in the saddle and ride mankind." Yet never did his words seem more apt than in 2020. All over the world people found themselves deeply changed by huge global forces over which we had no control.

In late February, Jim and I stopped leaving the house except for essentials. The Canadian border closed, band jobs were canceled, and by the end of March, we were in lockdown. All of the glories I had taken for granted—family dinners, dancing to Jim's bands, farmer's markets, and simply moving around the world freely—all that was gone.

The streets grew quieter, birdsong sounded louder. Thank goodness, the juncos and cardinals could not get the virus. All the gyms closed, and suddenly Holmes Dam was crowded with exercisers. I masked up and walked around the lake on icy paths with my friends. I felt grateful.

We lived between our city's two main hospitals, and overhead Jim and I saw and heard helicopters flying in COVID-19 patients from the little hospitals around the state. All day long sirens sounded as ambulances raced patients to emergency rooms, their red and blue lights flashing across the lake. At night, watching the stars and moon, we could see the lights of helicopters blink across the eastern sky toward St. Elizabeth's or Bryan Hospital.

As activities fell away, so did my sense of self. I had always defined myself by my relationships. Now everyone but Jim seemed far away. My life divided into two parts—before and after the pandemic. The time before became blurry and unreal, while the COVID-19 era seemed endless.

I knew I was one of the fortunate ones who did not need to work or worry about being evicted. I had tremendous respect for those who managed to carry on in spite of terrible difficulties. Their burdens were greater than mine, yet I still felt burdened.

At some point, a friend asked me what my plans were for the future. I was stupefied by the question and finally said, "We're having enchiladas for dinner."

The darkness descended on me like storm clouds, and some of these clouds didn't disperse for over a year. Like the year in that Ozark trailer, I was again unable to see my family. When I thought of the children in Canada, my body felt encased in ice.

There was no way to think about the future. No matter his or her expertise or power, no one really knew what would happen next. We could plan for nothing. The word for 2020 was surrender. Surrender your plans, your wishes, and your sense of agency. Keep your expectations low.

Gradually I began to respond more adaptively to our lockdown and our collective fears. I decided to spend the year reading about the history and literature of Black Americans. I signed a contract to write a new book, and I set up Zoom meetings with my environmental group.

As always, my women friends helped me hold my life in place. I walked almost every day with one friend or another. My writer's group had regular meetings online, and I had long calls with my family and friends in distant places.

Jim and I had never spent so much time together. We played Scrabble and watched comedies on television. In the evenings, with little to say about our days, we invented a happy game called "Do you remember?" One night it might be, "Do you remember all the times we visited a beach?" The next, we would ask, "What were the names of all our friends in graduate school?"

Over time we grew to be kinder and gentler with each other. We were two playing cards, holding each other upright. If we weren't happy with each other, we were not happy. So we rose to the occasion and became a more loving version of our former selves.

Small pleasures became big pleasures. My mantra was "Notice this moment." Notice reading by the fire as the snow falls, or Leonard Cohen songs playing on the radio, or drawing with my grandson on FaceTime. The lights of ambulances and helicopters were omnipresent, but I had ways to find other kinds of light.

Buddha Light

Before the pandemic, our sangha met on Sunday mornings in the basement of a psychologist's office. Often, I would rush across town and race into the meeting frazzled about my Sunday to-do list. However, as soon as I entered the sangha, my breathing would deepen and slow down.

In the middle of the meditation room, we spread out an ornate circle of Indian cloth and created a sacred area with flowers, candles, and a small statue of the Buddha. We sat around this circle on cushions or chairs.

Our meetings opened with check-in, then we meditated in silence for forty minutes. During the walking meditation, we slowly circled the room in our stocking feet, breathing in as we lifted a foot, breathing out as we set it down.

On the cushion, my mind raced. Every recent thought, from my grocery list to my interactions, recycled in some form. I worried if I had offended anyone.

I worked myself up about my responsibilities and questioned how I could do everything on my schedule. I missed my family. I wanted more of this, less of that. I berated myself for perceived shortcomings and mistakes.

Eventually though, my breathing became deeper and slower. And every now and then, I inhabited my body. I attended my tight scalp, my aching shoulders. I softened my jaw and relaxed the muscles around my eyes. I heard my beating heart and the wind outside. Thoughts and feelings still arose, but I didn't hold on to them. I observed them, let them float by, and returned to my breathing.

In meditation, I was lucky if I felt fully awake and conscious for one minute, but that moment was worth the effort. Sometimes I was even able to grant myself mercy and to smile at my foibles. Often life felt so precious that tears slid down my cheeks. I thought/felt, The universe is just so touching.

When meditation ended, I was no longer in just my ruminations or in, as Michael Pollan called it, my "default mode functioning." I had quieted my small ego-bound self and been in touch with something larger. My shoulders had softened, and my mind was now slow and relaxed. I no longer was holding on tight.

After meditation, we listened to dharma talks or shared our writing and art. Members led tea ceremonies or discussions. We ended our meetings with group hugs, and I walked out into the sunlight with a heart filled with love for the group and the world. I was no longer in a hurry.

With the pandemic, our group moved online. At first, I missed the candles, flowers, and the group hugs. However, in lockdown, I was grateful for the conversation and loving companionship of our sangha.

On Zoom sangha, we became larger and more diverse. Listening to others talk, I learned about their fears of poverty, their struggles to work with children at home, and their loneliness as single people, or parents or grandparents with children far away. And just by listening, I felt less isolated and lonely. My pain was shared pain. It was human pain.

We were staying alive and sane to help one another stay alive and sane. We became one another's life preservers.

When it was my turn to lead a meditation, I often guided the group in an exercise in which we were permeated from head to toe with a golden ball of light. As it spread through our bodies, we were warmed, calmed, and filled with love. Boundaries between ourselves and the "outside world" dissolved. We were in an interconnected web of consciousness.

When the morning sangha ended, I was already at home, in my living room on our worn couch with my old calico Glessie on my lap. I had once again discovered the golden light that is always within us. Nothing had changed and everything had changed.

Morel Hunting

On a beautiful day in May, Jim and I drove to Zeke's land along the Platte River. We had not seen our son's family since October of the year before. We were joyful at the thought of being outdoors with Zeke, Jamie, and the children.

We were on our way to hunt morels. These are deeply grooved conical mushrooms that surface for only a couple of weeks a year. They arrive with the lilacs, after a rain, when the sun bursts out and the weather heats up. They grow only in certain locations, usually near a river and close to oak or ash trees. If foragers are lucky enough to find a location for morels, they keep it to themselves. They would no more reveal their site's location than a fisherman would reveal his best fishing spot.

For years, I had yearned to find morels in the wild. I had searched for them in state parks and in the Ozarks with my cousin Steve, but I had never discovered one.

I would occasionally buy morels at farmer's markets—twenty-five dollars for eight ounces. Pan-fried in butter, they are meaty, with a robust, complex flavor. They taste like ancient deep forests, rain and soil, like something that has been here long before humans became a species. When I eat them, I am tasting time.

At the river, Zeke's family awaited us. Zeke handed us all mesh bags so that, as we picked and carried morels, we would be dispersing their spores. We headed into the woods along a bowered path. The newly leafing cottonwoods and oaks swayed in the breeze. The earth smelled green and loamy. Nearby a thrasher was running through her repertoire of cheerful melodies

We passed a beaver dam, and Zeke told me that beavers are such communal animals that when they are isolated, they stop eating and slowly shut down.

"Yes," I said, "I can believe that."

We walked by the spring-fed pond covered in duckweed. With every step, frogs jumped ahead of us and plunked into the water. The wild violets bloomed and the sun sparkled through the dappled light of freshly leafed trees. That's how my heart felt, sparkly.

Zeke bounded ahead like a deer. Jamie warned us of poison oak and scratchy berry bushes. Kate gathered me a bouquet of golden tickseed and phlox. Claire scanned the forest floor for the first sign of a morel. These mushrooms are hard to spot, especially if you've never seen one in the wild. They hide under dry leaves and range in color from tan to orange to black. Some are the size of almonds, others as big as apples.

"Mom, come over here," Zeke called out.

I ran up to him and looked where he was pointing. Below me in a patch of sunlight, a dozen morels awaited. "Oh my. Oh, my."

Jamie filmed as I stooped down to cut my first wild morels. I felt as if I had spotted a whooping crane or stumbled into a glade filled with rare fringed prairie orchids.

We continued on. We are a competitive family, and there were shouts, "I spotted that first" or "Wait, that's my patch." But also, family members often called to me, the slowest and most sight-impaired member, "Come over here. I found some for you to pick."

We were on the same intermittent reinforcement schedule that keeps fishermen fishing or gamblers gambling. Every now and then a deer would bound by us with the same enthusiasm as my son.

By the time we reached the Platte we had two pounds of morels, distributed more or less evenly across the six bags. Zeke invited us to his place where he could grill the morels outside and we could eat in our lawn chairs.

For a long time we sat by the river, basking in sunlight and fresh air. Looking down the banks and across the mile-wide Platte, we could only see the muddy river, full of Colorado snowmelt, the blue sky, the woods on the other side, and the komorebi of light in the trees beside us. It was just our family and the occasional blue heron or pelican. After so many months of separation and sorrow, everything made me laugh. I was drunk on happiness.

What more can I say about an oasis of joy, a balm in Gilead, and a spring day after a winter of despair. I will only say this. It was a form of rescue and repair.

Sunset

After dinner on summer evenings, I stay outside until it is dark. Sometimes, I garden or read in my hammock. Other nights I just watch the light change and listen to the sounds of day quieting down.

My backyard view suits me as much as any on earth. In the north, hydrangeas rise as tall as small trees. Red, white, and pink hibiscus as big as dinner plates are banked below. Looking west, I watch how sunlight filigrees the leaves on my Korean spice viburnum and forsythia. Behind them stately white pines stand against an old wooden fence. The way the light sifts through these pines at sunset astonishes me. As the colors of the sky change, so does this light, filtered through pine needles, from almost clear to lemon to as soft and golden as melted butter.

The cardinals and jays settle in for the night. The swallows stop diving for mosquitos and return to their nests above our garage. Last to quiet down are the wrens nesting in our ancient crabapple tree. They stop chattering at precisely the minute the sun fades from view. A few moments later I hear the barn owls and the scree-scree of bats.

A peace falls over the land and all of us animals upon it. I drink in this peace, this beauty as if it were fine champagne. My cares of the day, the events from the news cycle, and even my restlessness all fade away. My tense shoulders relax. The sunset may be the greatest tranquilizer ever created. But, unlike medications, it leaves us alert and relaxed.

We humans have always watched the sun go down. No matter our circumstance, we could count on a blaze of glory at the end of most days. The sun is democratic and spends itself for all of us.

Over the years, I have watched the sunsets with my grandmothers, my Ozark relatives, my siblings, my parents, my friends, my children, and my grandchildren. I've watched it sink below horizons in Capetown, Warsaw, Okinawa, and Chiang Mai. I've seen it drop behind mountains in the Rockies and the Sierra Nevadas, and I've watched thousands of sunsets on the plains of Nebraska.

I watch it now, as an old woman with my brothers far away and my family grown and living in other towns.

Maybe old age is when many of us love the sunset most. We lose people, and life crushes us in its various ways. Hope can seem like a dark star in another solar system. Yet, every night, the sun once again offers us all that it has. It whispers, "Take these coins of gold, these shafts of light, and these pink and orange silk scarves of sky."

The Perseids

In mid-August Jim and I drove northwest into the Sandhills of Nebraska to watch the Perseids meteor shower. With less than one person per square mile, this area has some of the best stargazing in the world, and astronomy groups hold their meetings there. For many Americans, Nebraska is either a flyover state or a place to cross on I-80 to get to someplace prettier. Off the interstate, what makes Nebraska grand is its emptiness, especially in the Sandhills. The sky is its Rocky Mountains.

We drove through the sage green hills that resemble ocean waves. The only human-made structures we saw were battered old windmills, falling-down barns, and round loaves of hay. Occasionally we spotted a man on a tractor cutting alfalfa or brome. Sunflowers filled the ditches and scrub cedars dotted the hills.

Frequently we noted a lone hardwood tree in the middle of an expanse of land. These trees always touch my heart. They stand as a metaphor for something—our essential loneliness or our endurance.

As evening came, the shadows from the trees and the haystacks lengthened. The hills themselves cast long blue shadows. Five baby pheasants skittered across the road in front of us.

We drove through the almost empty towns until we reached Broken Bow. It was the last "big town" before the national forest in Halsey. Next to the scrap-iron dinosaur statue at the Boneyard Creation Museum sat a Dollar General. The Arrow Inn, the historic three-story stone hotel downtown, had a sign that said, "Sturgis Bikers welcome here."

As we neared our destination, we stopped talking and just gathered it all in. There is a sacred quality to these hills, especially near sunset. We imbibed the calm beauty of this place.

We passed through Halsey, population seventy-six, and into the twenty-two-thousand-acre forest. We crossed the Dismal River and drove alongside the Middle Loup, a wide brown river that meanders through the area.

We chose a campsite and set up our tent. Jim built a big fire with pine cones and firewood. As we waited for the sunlight to fade, we watched the firelight dance and sway in her many-colored gowns.

Campfires tell a long story that goes back to the ancient ones who first discovered how to build fires.

I could feel the bones of my ancestors in the embers' glow. Their lives burned before me as mine will before my descendants. How beautifully the flames disappeared into the darkness.

I didn't know how much I needed the smell of wood smoke, the calls of the nighthawks, the mercy of trees, and the murmur of a river.

As we watched the fire, we heard an ethereal high-pitched cry from nearby. At first, we thought it might be a coyote or a fox, but as the pitch grew higher, we realized it was a screech owl. Deep in the forest another owl responded. Their duet sent shivers up my spine.

Around eleven, we lay down on a road not far from our campsite, away from the trees, in order to see the full sky. Far from the fire, the air was chill, but the asphalt was still warm and soft, as if we were lying on a geothermal carpet. We heard crickets and, from a distance, Mr. Buffett's coal trains moving east.

The night sky changed my breathing. The stars were close and liquid. I felt that if I climbed a tree, I could touch them. The Milky Way was as malt-like as it was when I was a young girl. Cassiopeia, the Big Dipper, the North Star, and the Pleiades were surrounded by so many stars that they actually were harder to distinguish than the stars in the city. When a fireball fell from the crown of the sky, we felt as if it might hit us in the face.

I was a fleck of dust in an enormous universe, fortunate to even exist. Our lives are as fragile as the smallest
falling star that flashes across the dome of night. We
blaze for a moment and then we are gone.

Strawberry Moon

After a month of record heat, Lincoln had its first cool evening. It was Sunday just after sunset, a full moon was rising, and I was free to treat myself to an evening outside moon watching.

I sat in my lawn chair and inhaled deep, exhaled slowly. The air smelled of grass, grain, and roses. The cicadas sang all around me. I could hear people walking on the dam and traffic noise from twelve blocks away. On the lake, three fishing boats, each with a small white light, rocked gently on the small waves.

Just above the horizon, the moon was red from the fires in Colorado and California. In San Francisco the air was so thick with smoke and the temperatures were so high that, to keep cool, my brother sat in front of a fan in his underwear with cold towels on his body. Jake had COPD, and he was struggling to breathe. Tonight

I wished he were here with me at the end of a cool, green day.

Bats and swallows were hunting mosquitos. Peepers called out from the lake. Our resident barn owl cruised from the masthead pine to a white pine in the west. Geese flew onto the lake and squabbled for a few minutes before settling down for the night.

A few stars blinked on, and the now silver moon rose over the pines across the lake. She cast a silver beam that one of the little fishing boats drifted across.

Before the pandemic I had never felt old. Because Jim was a musician, I had spent many nights dancing and seeing my friends. Grandchildren had been in our pool almost every afternoon, and visitors from the coasts had come and gone all summer long. With the pandemic, I had thrown my expectations like confetti into the wind.

Just this summer Jim and I had hoped to visit our old friends Frank and Frances in Scotland. Frank's health was fading, and we wanted to enjoy a week with him before he was gone. But, of course, these trips didn't happen. COVID summer, lonely summer.

My life had become a much smaller life.

Yet this summer had its share of joys. My granddaughter Kate worked in Lincoln on Tuesdays, and around five P.M., she showed up at our place. She would swim and then we would order Chinese takeout. Her bright energy changed my moods. Kate left only in time to drive the ninety minutes to her home before dark.

My friend Jan baked me lavender scones. I swam every day and walked in the early morning with women friends. I read outside in my hammock and worked in the garden. Day by day, I was mostly happy. I knew how privileged I was to be healthy, on Medicare, with a home near a park.

August was the peak of our time with animals. The orioles, meadowlarks, and red-winged blackbirds were here and also the frogs, turtles, and cicadas. Sometimes we had a mink in our backyard, and we would catch a glimpse of coyotes. I could often hear foxes calling in the distance. That awakened something wild and free in me.

August was the month of tomatoes, eggplant, basil, peppers, and pears. My yard groaned with abundance, but soon fall would be here. Usually I looked forward to the seasons changing, but I pictured ahead holidays alone, months away from loved ones, and the absence of outings. I hoped I would be strong enough to find some fun. I was frightened I wouldn't be.

I was sitting outside, and eventually the crimson moon worked her magic on me. Moonlight cooled my fevered mind and bathed me in peace.

Many of the happiest moments in my life had come when I paid attention to the moon. It was as hypnotic as the face of a newborn baby.

"Dear Grandmother Moon, how I love thee. I thank you for your luminescent kindness and cooling energy. And Mother Earth, I love you too. Thank you for the smell of tomato plants, the happy chattering of the wrens and the caressing breeze. Over and over, you both have saved me from heartbreak. I know you will be with me when winter comes, and forever after."

Prairie Grasses

On Thanksgiving I had a hard time facing the morning. I remembered previous years with a house full of family, babies to rock, and young ones to "help" me cook. I could picture our big table with flowers, homemade bread, wine bottles, and sippy cups. I thought about our after-dinner charades where even the youngest children took a turn and about how we adults talked by the fire far into the night.

This year I wouldn't pull out the leaves of my big table, polish the champagne glasses, or buy a big turkey. This year there were cobwebs on Otis's orange plastic truck. We FaceTimed with the children, but Jim and I dined alone.

After a cup of coffee and some attitude adjustment, I stopped pondering what I didn't have and considered what I did. I had plenty—a warm house, a nearby lake, good health, and Jim.

All morning Jim and I called couples we hadn't seen in this year of no travel. Most of them were older, and, like us, they were alone for the holiday. Our conversations were jovial and laced with laughter and affection. We promised to visit the minute the vaccines arrived. These calls reminded us that even if we could not be with our friends, we were connected to people we loved.

Later Jim and I drove out to Audubon Spring Creek Prairie. It was a sunny, fifty-degree day. Good walking weather. The nature center was closed, but the gate was open and we had the place to ourselves.

Walking on this prairie is to walk back in time. It's the largest tract of tall grass prairie in Nebraska, and it has never been plowed. We passed rocks pushed into the Great Plains as glacial till. Around the biggest rocks, buffalos once circled and scratched themselves, leaving behind dry moats called buffalo wallows. We traversed the ruts from Conestoga wagons as they crossed this land on the Nebraska-Fort Kearny Cutoff of the Oregon Trail.

We wandered through the old-growth forest of burr oaks, whose limbs were as twisted and intertwined as wicker baskets. The wind played a scratchy sonata as it moved through the branches and the big limbs creaked and groaned. A red-tailed hawk hunted overhead.

We hiked the open prairie—miles of rolling hills covered by indigenous grasses under a big sky. Without roads, cultivated land, electric lines, or buildings in our sight lines, we could pretend we lived long ago when the land belonged to the indigenous peoples, and buffalo and bear crossed this prairie.

We topped the hills farthest from the nature center. From this vantage point we had watched prairie chickens do their mating dance. We could smell the sage amid the sea of grasses—big and little bluestem, Indian love grass, switchgrass, and sideoats grama, all intermingled with remnants of leadplant and prairie asters. Below us the blue pond sparkled in the bright sunlight, and the meadow was filled with the now leafless cottonwoods.

We saved our favorite part until the end. On the far western side of the prairie there was a stretch of scarlet big bluestem that measured over seven feet high. Jim and I loved to lose ourselves in this river of grass, to be surrounded by it and let it caress us as we moved through it.

We lay down and looked up seven feet through the red grass to the blue sky. Our loneliness disappeared in the suchness of the moment.

We watched the grass toss and sway above us and listened to the soft music of the wind. When Bob Dylan was asked the meaning of "Blowing in the Wind," he responded, "If you have ever really listened to the wind, you know what it's about. If you haven't, I can't explain it to you."

Listening to the wind I could hear time, geological time, plant and animal time, and indigenous peoples' time. I could hear the voices of my ancestors who made the great crossing from Scotland and Ireland to become the sodbusters of Nebraska. The wind carries the breath of all living creatures and the dust from the bones of the ancient ones, of my people and yours. Sometimes in it, I can hear weeping: other times I hear children playing and laughter.

There is nothing like lying on the ground to ground us. We feel the earth beneath us and look at the sky above. We are no longer a small individual being but are connected to the great suchness of the universe.

Musical Light

When my grandson Coltrane was three, I picked him up from his preschool to drive him to our house. After I belted him into his industrial-strength car seat in the back, I turned on NPR. A Bach sonata for violin was playing. At various moments in this piece, when he was moved by the music, I heard Coltrane whispering, "Beautiful . . . Beautiful."

On Christmas morning, the year Coltrane turned five, we were at his house by seven A.M. John, Sara, Jim, and I followed Coltrane as he walked to the basement for his last gift from Santa. When he spotted a full drum set awaiting him, he froze for a moment before bounding to it.

Dressed only in his Superman pajama bottoms, he sat down to play. We adults drank coffee and watched him as he carefully tested out the snare, the cymbals, and the high hat. Then we listened to his first "practice." That year, he played his drum set for hours every day.

The next year Jim bought him an electronic keyboard. When he visited us, he would dash straight to it. Sometimes he chorded or drummed along with the recorded melodies; other times, he sounded out tunes for himself or composed music. He had taken Suzuki piano in Lincoln, and later a few lessons in Canada, but he was mostly self-taught.

When I asked Coltrane about his musical influences, he said, "My dad introduced me to music, but Mom introduced me to music I liked."

Now, at eleven, Coltrane works with a keyboard, Garage Band, and FL Studio Mobile. He has learned a great deal more about composing and arranging. With that technology he can download any song he wants off the internet, then edit it and add track after track of different instruments.

On one of our visits to Canada, Coltrane offered to teach me the chords to Coldplay's song "The Scientist." Because I am both uncoordinated and tone-deaf, I was reluctant to even try. However, Coltrane was persistent and insistent, and I eventually agreed. He painstakingly taught me how to chord the song. Several times, I would say, "I give up." He would respond, "Nonna, you can do it, please."

After many trials, I could do it. While I nervously chorded along, Coltrane stood beside me belting out the lyrics. "I had to find you/Tell you I need you/Tell you I set you apart."

Coltrane has a high tenor voice, and he poured his heart into the song. If he had been Paul McCartney and I had played first violin in the London Symphony Orchestra, I couldn't have been prouder of us.

One morning in December, we were on FaceTime, and I asked him to play me some music. COVID-19 was at an all-time high in both of our countries. His province was in strict lockdown, and he couldn't see friends, attend school, or go on outings.

Coltrane sat on his unmade bed in a Hogwarts sweatshirt with his blond hair cascading across his face. First, he played me a song he had reworked—"Piece of Your Heart," by Meduza featuring Goodboys. His version sounded like bullfrog with lots of drums and bass. At a certain moment he said, "Nonna, here's the drop." Later I asked him what "drop" meant. He said, "It's the moment where all the elements of the song come together."

As I listened to Coltrane play, I was aware that he was fifteen hundred miles away and I hadn't seen him in over a year. I had no idea when I would see him. He was changing daily, and I was missing almost all those changes. Missing my grandchildren as they have grown created considerable darkness in my life.

Losing children is as hard as losing parents, but it happens all the time. Our own children leave us when they grow up, but even before that, we lose the three-year-old child when he or she turns four. Fortunately, these children usually return, not the same children who left, but still with the power to engolden our hearts.

When Coltrane plays music, my life brightens up. I feel the glow in my heart that comes with a deep connection to those I love. My life does a "drop," and, for one moment, all the elements of my universe come together in perfect synchrony. "Beautiful . . . Beautiful."

Rescue

On the darkest night of the darkest year of our century, I watched geese circle, set their wings, and land on the pink sunset ice on Holmes Lake. I felt as fragile as a Fabergé egg. Even the creamsicle-colored sky couldn't fix me.

I had been reading reports of the new more infectious variant of the coronavirus that was shutting down London and southeast England. My heart ached for all the pain and sorrow in the world.

I was missing my children and grandchildren, who I would not see this holiday season. And, in the last week, I cracked my ribs during a fall on the icy trails around the lake and heard of a friend's suicide. I felt "squishy." I was a plane that could not rise above dense fog into the sunlight. Some days I was literally seeping sorrow.

Fortunately, Jim suggested we drive around town to look for holiday lights. We drove slowly toward our old neighborhood where we had raised our children. A half moon hung silver above us and Orion lay on the eastern horizon. In the southwest sky, Saturn and Mercury had almost connected into one fireball.

In one yard, flashing green lights filled the trees. In another the lights were sparkling white, and, in yet another, colored lights blanketed the trees. I especially loved the tall pines adorned with jewel-colored lights. Their branches reached out to offer me beauty. "Here," they whispered, "take this into your heart."

We drove past diamond deer and bushes enrobed with lights sparkling through the snow. Many houses had a new kind of display that caused snowflakes to splash down garages and across lawns. Jim slowed so that I could be showered with those mother-of-pearl snowflakes.

Some of the old three-story houses had windows full of electric candles. Other windows heralded, with their family Christmas trees, "There is joy in this house. And celebration."

My favorite color for lights is blue, and, every now and then, we would see blue lights sparkling far into the tops of trees. As we drove home, I saw tall oaks, their arms lit by multicolored lights that seemed to fall like stars from the sky. The brightly colored pieces of light fell through the branches onto the snow and right into me. The more difficult the times, the more we need ecstasy. Jim stopped the car, I stepped outside, and I opened up my dark heart to let that rainbow of light pour in.

VIII

Wisdom Light

Will They Remember?

Will my grandchildren remember how when they were babies, I carried them outside to look at the sky and the green, how I tickled their faces with flowers and blew dandelion fluff for them to watch? How I held their hands up against tree bark and fern and dipped their toes in rainwater?

Will their bodies recall the back and forth of our ancient wooden rocker? Or our afternoons reading books as we swayed in the hammock under the pines? Once, I read Kate twenty-six books, and, when I finished, she asked me to do it again.

Will the children retain the feel of my arms around them as I carried them about the house pointing at objects and saying, "Book. Kitty. Banana."

When they change their own children's diapers, will they sing show tunes to keep them from wriggling away? When they feed their babies, will they call out the rhyme

I sang to them, "Open your mouth and shut your eyes and I'll give you something to make you wise."

Will they remember the summer nights when they woke at three A.M. and I carried them outside? How we lay on a blanket and I told them stories about the stars?

Or how Jim and I gave each of them a bird guide for their second birthdays and spent hours looking at those books and playing birdsongs on our IdentiFlyer?

Will they recall how we would all take paper bags for our nature walks? How we picked up bright leaves, pretty rocks, acorns, and seedpods? And how we made little necklaces from clover?

Can they envision us turning over rocks and looking for roly-polies, crickets, or millipedes? Or how, with our butterfly nets, we caught katydids and grasshoppers in the meadow? We would put them in a jar with airholes and look them up on the computer. That is, we did this until we injured a grasshopper. Then Coltrane said, "Let's not do that anymore."

Does he remember that day?

Will they remember that all of our wild animals had names? Our mallard pair, Cinnamon and Mint? Our possums, Blinky and Sparkle?

Will the children recall our cooking lessons? How they stood on their special stools and I taught them how to fill a pitcher with water and drop in four teabags? How, after sun tea, they learned to mix fruit salad and to make guacamole? Will they remember the face toast we made with raisins and dried apricots? Or how the shrimp chips from the Vietnamese grocery exploded into colored flowers in the hot oil?

Will they remember the patient old veteran who sold rocks at the farmer's market? How, before they spent their dollar on a small bag of their favorites, he let them hold and play with the rocks for as long as they wanted?

Or how on August afternoons, Jim climbed high in our trees and dropped down peaches? And how we all ran under the tree trying to catch them in butterfly nets?

Will the children remember the stories I told of the Lovelies and the McGarigles, two families who epitomized the extremes of comportment? How whenever we did something for the first time such as go to a museum or play miniature golf, I would tell of the naughty McGarigles who demonstrated every form of inappropriate behavior, and then of the Lovelies who knew how to act properly?

Will they remember rolling walnuts down our hill to see whose was the fastest? Or playing hide-and-seek outside with lightning bugs twinkling around us?

And will they remember paddling about the swimming pool? Will they recall how I picked fresh raspberries and dropped them into their mouths as if they were goldfish? Or how I pretended to be a customer at their outdoor restaurant, and they bungled all my orders so we could laugh at the ketchup in coffee or the ice cream sundae with spinach on top?

How could they forget the Popsicle parties with our towels wrapped around us and the sunlight shining through the pines and straight onto our shivering limbs? Or how, after our swims, we had flower fights with withering hibiscus blossoms? We would each have a small pile, and, at the count of three, we would bombard each other with the soft flowers.

Will they hold in their hearts those summer days when we were all together with the sun high in the sky and the water sparkling in the pool?

Will they recall that everything we did was so sacred it became a ritual?

And, how much does it matter that they remember?

I remember every one of these things and many more.

Winter Moon

At sunset on New Year's Day, Jim and I walked on Holmes Dam. The winter sky was silver and pink, and long blue shadows fell across the snow. We could hear the soundtrack of winter, geese flying overhead in search of open waters. Skaters and ice fisherman dotted the lake. Sledding children with their bright coats and boots covered the dam like confetti.

We watched one little boy with a red cap who, after sliding down the steep incline of the dam, refused to stand up. His dad picked up his sled, checked that he was not hurt and offered him a hand up, but the boy shook his head and turned away. The dad shrugged his shoulders and dashed up the dam for another run. Other sledders whizzed by the boy, then jumped up and trudged back to the top. The boy just lay in the snow wriggling and fussing, making a show of needing help.

This scene reminded me of an incident earlier in the week. At dusk, just as Jim and I were having our nightly glass of wine, we heard sirens coming from all directions. Flashing red and blue lights converged across the lake. We counted nine rescue vehicles, including ambulances, fire trucks, and police. We could see just well enough to make out people, some with stretchers and ropes, running toward the lake. It looked like a fisherman had fallen through the ice and was clinging to a small shelf waiting to be rescued. Sadly, it was too dark for us to see what happened in the icy water. One by one the vehicles left the area. Jim noted that no sirens were sounding or lights flashing, and we wondered if that meant the man had died.

I pondered those two incidents as I watched the almost full apricot moon rise over the icy lake and snow-covered land. It turned out that both stories ended well. Eventually, the little boy stood up, a pudgy Frosty in his red hat. He dusted himself off and plowed through the snow toward his family. The man who fell through the ice was rushed to the hospital with hypothermia, but he survived to fish another day.

Somehow both the little boy and the freezing man seemed like metaphors for something, maybe something no more complicated than "Life is a struggle." Or perhaps the metaphor is this, "We are all waiting to be rescued."

While I could identify with both the fallen boy and the fisherman, perhaps instead I was one of the sledders, hurling myself down, faster and faster into something new and marvelous.

Recently my granddaughter had asked me to take her to Europe when the pandemic was over. "Of course I will, if I can outlive it."

Someday I will take Kate to bookstores in Paris and London, and we'll dine on croissants and scones. We'll walk along the Seine and the Thames and visit the British Museum and Versailles.

However, right now, the moonlight gliding on ice is a form of rescue. We sit together, the moon and I, until only the moon remains.

Wisdom Light

In mid-February 2021, all the suffering of the past year came to a head. Perhaps it was the lack of vaccines and the warnings of dangerous virus mutations, plus the second impeachment trial of Donald Trump. Add a year of isolation coupled with twenty inches of snow and days with highs of minus five. Cap the whole catastrophic month off with my grandson Otis turning seven. We had a virtual birthday party, but I was aware that we had missed his entire sixth year.

I had been grieving and yearning, wanting my family so badly my heart hurt. A part of me had been hibernating, just waiting for contact with my children and grandchildren to wake me up.

Then one day, as I sat drinking my first cup of coffee, from a place deep within, from my heart/mind, a voice cried out, "Enough."

"Enough making yourself miserable. Enough placing the power to be happy in your children's hands, enough having a heart in three different places. Enough waiting for reunion. Be happy now. Be happy here. Life is good."

Later, as I meditated, I was aware of my beating heart. How grateful I was for its steady pulse. How deeply I realized that when my heart stopped beating I would be finished.

I contemplated what Buddhists call the three poisons—anger, ignorance, and attachment. I had always understood the dangers of ignorance and anger, but attachment as a poison was hard for me to understand.

Isn't attachment another word for love, something I had been seeking all of my life? Wasn't I happy when I felt loved? However, the Buddhist meaning of attachment applies to any emotions that leave us wanting and yearning. Now at last I understood that my love for my children and grandchildren, my missing them constantly, had caused me to suffer. What could save me was loosening my grip and surrendering to the situation I could not change.

On the next Sunday, the third day of the Lunar New Year, I heard a story about the Buddha. He was sitting under a tree with his followers when a farmer approached and asked him if he had seen six lost cows. The Buddha had not, but he asked his followers if they had seen the cows. All shook their heads no. The man burst into tears and ran off shouting, "I am ruined. Those cows were all I had."

The Buddha turned to his followers and said, "Consider your good fortune. You have no cows to lose."

I needed to relinquish my cows.

I had no time to waste. On the contrary, I wanted to be grateful for every day. My misery about my faraway children would end only if I ended it. Sara's family wasn't moving back to Nebraska. Kate was already away at college and by next September Aidan would be too. Claire was a junior and busy with sports and work. Five young children would never again surround me in the swimming pool. I was no longer a central figure in anyone's life but Jim's. He and I would be mostly by ourselves from now on and then one day one of us would be alone.

Everything is process and in process. We can hold on to nothing.

I once told a friend, "Life is fundamentally tragic." She responded, "No, it is fundamentally impermanent." That has been a hard lesson to accept.

I've found it difficult to accept a cycle of life in which children grow up and leave their parents, and in which we parents become more and more peripheral. When I was with my family they had been my greatest joy, but needing and wanting them had been punishing.

Connection to me had always felt like a life-or-death matter. However, I was no longer in a trailer without my mother or alone in a hospital with a doctor who forced me to take a shot. I could choose to stop making myself unhappy by waiting for something that would never happen. I could declare a truce with my own neediness and simply walk away from it. I could end my argument with reality and accept life as it is. This heart/mind insight comforted me.

As adults, we never manage to meet our unmet childhood needs. We can't even meet all the needs we have in the present. However, we can acquire the skills to redefine many of our needs as wants. We can be happy only if we know what to want.

When this revelation came to me, I felt a great release. Tension flowed out my body and my breathing became deeper and slower. Over the next few days I noticed how much lighter I felt. I stopped having nightmares about being lost, left behind, or dislocated from my home. I ceased waiting. More often, I was present with the days. I was accepting impermanence and moving in gratitude for what was present. I had released my cows.

At least for the moment.

We never stop having lessons in impermanence.

My Son's Kitchen

Two weeks after our second vaccination, Jim and I drove ninety miles west to celebrate our son's fiftieth birthday. We had visited Zeke and his family outside during the summer of 2020, but this was the first time we would be able to hug them and have dinner inside their house.

We all had lost people we loved in the last year, and Jamie and Zeke had been ill with COVID-19. But now we were taking brie and fresh fish for Zeke to grill. We were reuniting.

When we arrived, Jamie and Zeke came out to welcome us. We hugged, longer and tighter than in the past. Then we followed our traditional routines. We examined the garden and found the first nubs of asparagus popping up. The rhubarb plants were already bursting forth in their red and green colors.

Beside their empty chicken shed, we checked out the raspberry vines that we had transplanted from our yard to theirs. Standing in the yard talking in the new green spring, I took nothing for granted. I had waited a long time for this moment and now it was here. My blood felt as if it were made of champagne, and I had a big goofy grin that I didn't even try to disguise. The slant of the sun etched everything with gold.

When Claire and Aidan came home from track practice, they were almost shy with us. Aidan was taller than Jim now and muscular from school sports and his construction job. Claire's blond hair had darkened and she wore it in a braided bun. She was over six feet tall, taller than either her brother or sister, and she looked more like a young woman than the girl we had last visited.

Soon we were sitting around the kitchen island watching Zeke and Jamie prepare dinner. Claire sat beside me and, every few minutes, leaned in for another hug. Zeke coated the fish in spices and chopped up vegetables for a salad. It was both familiar and magical. I was back in real life unmediated by screens and devices and, once again, could live in the vibrant stream of the senses.

Aidan told us of his decision to go to college in Denver. We talked about the outdoor fun he could have in the mountains—hiking, fly-fishing, and snowboarding. I told him that when we came to visit we would go to the

Brown Palace Hotel for a meal. He could wear the blue suit he had purchased for graduation.

At dinner, Zeke said grace. He thanked God we could be together. "Amen," I said, "Amen."

We kept holding hands and looked around the table at one another's radiant faces. Then Jamie passed the salad and Aidan lifted the heavy fish platter. We laughed and joked our way through dinner. So ordinary. So wonderful.

After the meal Jamie carried in an Earl Grey cake with five tall golden candles. After we sang "Happy Birthday," we had our own tradition. We each said a word that described the birthday person. When we finished, Zeke had tears in our eyes.

We said our goodbyes early. It was midweek, and the children needed to study. We made the long drive home, tired and happy. I had long believed *home* was the most beautiful word in the English language, but now I decided that it was *reunion*. Perhaps they are the same word.

Of course, I love my son and his family and feel a warm glow of connection when we are together. However, the time I spend with them is only a small part of my life. When Jim and I say goodbye, we return to our lives and they rapidly spin out into a very different solar system than our own. Reunions are a both/and experience. I both celebrate the relationships and realize that soon we will be parting. There is another beautiful word in our language. That word is *acceptance*.

The Cranebow

On a windy March day, Jim and I packed for our annual pilgrimage to the sandhill crane migration. We loaded up binoculars, boots, and winter coats. I packed a picnic with fresh raspberries and chocolate chip cookies for dessert.

After a week of rainfall, the sun was out. The fields and the trees were still browns and grays, but on the west side of the Blue River, farmers had planted winter wheat now shimmering green in the sun.

We drove past old farmsteads, their rusted windmills standing loyally beside the broken buildings. Many of the old settlers' barns were still upright, often with a tree growing through the erstwhile roofs. We passed little prairie graveyards, built 150 years ago by pioneer families. Old people and children, some of whom had never seen a city, were buried in these places. Big families of

Germans, Swedes, and Czechs once lived here. Every ruined homestead and graveyard had a story I longed to know.

After we passed the York exit, we played our usual game, "Who will see the first crane?"

Sandhill cranes are gray, tan, and white birds with a bright red spot on their heads. They grow to be four feet tall with a six-foot wingspread, but they are well camouflaged, easily fading into the brush, trees, and dull winter grasses. Cranes are hard to spot until you've done it a few times.

Every March for ten thousand years, these magnificent birds have journeyed along the hourglass-shaped Central Flyway of North America. The middle of that hourglass is a fifty-mile area along the Platte River about two hours from my home.

Jim spotted the first ones. They blanketed a field of corn stubble to our north. Every year we forget how stunned we will be when we spot them.

We turned off at the Alda exit and drove on country roads alongside the braided Platte. A palomino stood in a field dotted with hay bales shaped like loaves of bread. Newborn calves drank milk from their placid mothers. Cows, horses, and cranes lived in slow time, and attuning to their movements slowed me down.

The Platte was wide and muddy here, running fast with snowmelt. Ancient cottonwoods lined the river. Scrub cedars, with their strange rust-green hue, dotted the pastures. Rainwater the color of cocoa filled the ditches, but in the afternoon sunlight all water shone.

We stood in an outdoor theater with cranes surround-sound. Birds flew overhead calling from all directions. They seemed to purr, coo, and warble all at the same time. It's an ancient sound as wild and comforting as the sound of ocean waves.

We stopped at another field of cranes. The cranes flying overhead cast shadows across the stubble. When they landed, they glided in like airplanes, their wings set and their heads straight out. Their landings were bumpy and clumsy, as if their genetic code somehow doesn't contain landing instructions.

The wind was blowing, as it always is on the prairie, and, in spite of all our blankets and coats, we were soon chilled. But we stayed outside.

We pilgrims were at our holy site. Once again, we witnessed a miracle, absorbed in the immensity and mystery of it all. What we were seeing and hearing cannot be captured in mere words. It is bigger than language, bigger than us.

Late afternoon we parked our car along a dirt road a mile from Rowe Sanctuary. On our right we could see the Platte with its sandbars awaiting the cranes. The light in the cottonwoods along the riverbank sparkled the way cottonwoods always do in late afternoon. Somehow the sound of the river, the sound of the cottonwoods, and the sound of the cranes all became one sound.

I unpacked our picnic, and we enjoyed a feast at the best outdoor café in the world. On our left was a field full of cranes gathering before their sunset flight to the islands in the river. As we watched, hundreds of cranes dropped down. Many of them did their beautiful crane dance, which consists of leaping into the air and flapping their wings in unison with other cranes.

There was a moment when a crane was just landing, with its wings fully spread, becoming translucent. It turned into a crane-shaped form outlined by a thin line of mercury and infused with prismatic light. I beheld an illuminated crane-shaped rainbow, a "cranebow."

It happened so quickly, just for a millisecond, when the light caught its vast wingspread, just so. I could barely take it in before it disappeared. But that I had seen a "cranebow" was indisputable. This miracle, as evanescent as an eye blink, will stay in my memory forever.

I wondered, "Am I seeing these miracles because I am paying more attention, or is the great consciousness of the universe opening herself to me?"

The Light We Can Always Find

We are all palimpsests, our lives layered over the lives of ten thousand generations of ancestors, and, soon enough, we will join them. We inhabit bodies that carry all the trauma, happiness, defeat, and resilience of those who came before us. Within this variegated palette of the collective consciousness, we are born into a place and time.

From our genetics, circumstances, and choices, we develop an identity. I am made of the KOA fountain, snaky Ozark lakes, Beaver Creek, the Concordia sandpit, my son's ball games, my daughter's violin concerts, and scores of therapy clients. I embody all the music I have heard, all the books I have read. I contain Abe Lincoln, Willa Cather, Thich Nhat Hanh, and the Fabtones.

My story begins when I was a baby looking at dappled light through trees. As an infant and young girl, I was totally dependent on my family for love, but by the time I was ten I knew how to seek out loving people and create relationships. And I had learned to comfort myself with animals, rivers, and trees. Reading was also a great solace, my map of the world and the propellant of my moral imagination. And like many lonely children, I bonded with Mother Earth, Father Sky, and Grandmother Moon.

Now, in my eighth decade, I come as close as I can to my childhood patterns. I love to be with my family, and by now I have reunited with my daughter and her family. Once again we are able to get together for the family holidays I enjoy immensely, just as I did as a girl.

In the summer, I wake at dawn and go outside for my morning coffee. I watch the rabbits and squirrels at play. I see my friends and I swim. I am a huge fan of decks, porches, pergolas, and outdoor cafés. In the summer, I read in my hammock until it is so dark I can no longer decipher the words on the page. I still take great pleasure in dappled light in the trees.

I have been lucky. My life has been filled with good books, music, people, and the vast open land of Nebraska. I have wanted a life filled with love, and for the most part I've had it.

The pandemic took me to the heart of my loneliness. Events were out of my control in a way they hadn't been since I felt abandoned in a trailer in Missouri. At first, I was overwhelmed by lockdown isolation and, during the winter holidays, I was numb with grief. However, I knew I could no longer make my happiness dependent on external conditions. The only way forward was to grow.

Ordinary happiness depends on the circumstances of the day. We enjoy a walk with our dog or see a great movie. We fix a Cajun meal for our friends or go on a beach vacation. Deep happiness is independent of conditions. It is a matter of attention. The pandemic has been a great teacher. I have learned the true meaning of home: where we find the light when all grows dark.

No matter our circumstances, with effort, we can learn to control our attention. We can accept responsibility for our own happiness and look inside ourselves for the light we can always find. As a flourishing friend told me, "I have everything I need to be happy right between my ears."

I am no longer a child in a trailer waiting to be rescued or a girl alone in a hospital with a needle-wielding doctor. Now I am the age my mother was when she died, and like Archibald MacLeish's *J.B.*, based on the story of Job, I am learning to find light by "blowing on the coals of my heart."

I have learned to focus on every good thing that comes my way. I have lowered my expectations about what I can receive from the world and have stopped taking so much for granted. I have learned to surrender.

The lessons of my terrifying trip to Costa Rica returned to me. When I was weakening and drifting out to sea, surrender is what saved me. Coming to terms with fate is its own kind of salvation.

Our great challenge is coming to grips with impermanence. Fortunately, life is a great teacher and offers a continual lesson in loss. Sometimes I accept impermanence and sometimes I resist it. Mostly I lead a double life, happy day by day, but also aware of the tragedies we all carry.

Most days I can find light regardless of external conditions. I make an effort not to squander one precious minute. I can't allow my longing to cost me another day of my life.

I channel my grandmother who lived through the 1918 flu pandemic in a house with no running water and who survived the Dust Bowl, the Great Depression, and two world wars. She exemplified the phrase "making the best of it." Surprisingly, I live very much as she lived at my age. I have a garden, peach trees, my friends and family, and books.

Looking for the light does not mean denying the darkness. I try not to micromanage my feelings. If I am heartbroken, I let myself be heartbroken. If I am sad, angry, confused, or in despair, I allow myself to feel those emotions. That is the only way to be an honest, authentic person. But, even as I try to stay with pain, I also know that it will pass. Pain, like almost everything else, is impermanent.

Receiving love is impermanent, but giving love can be permanent. That is our good fortune. Margaret Mead wrote that "growing up means getting outside oneself and cherishing the life of the world." When we do this, we are primed for joy and amazement. We feel a great vibrancy as we face the critical challenges of the hour.

When I had the epiphany about "relinquishing my cows," I felt I had turned a corner. My husband jokes that I have turned so many corners I am going in circles, and he is partly right. However, I like to think the circles are spirals and that, over time, I have indeed become happier, calmer, and kinder to myself and others. That is all I can ask for.

Meditation and the mindfulness practices of my sangha have helped me stay present with sensory experience and attend the beauty around me. These practices have primed me for ecstatic experience. It also helps to be a developmental psychologist, since I know I am in a life stage when my growth involves relinquishing control.

Light is my intoxicant of choice. This morning, for example, the sun rose over the lake with its iridescent fog that was opal, then pink, and finally ice blue. With eyes wide open, everything is sacred.

Much of the time the world looks like a Monet painting. I bought a prism so that whenever the sun is out and at the right angle, I can go rainbow bathing. I look for the radiant light both outside and inside myself. That light helps me see that there is always a way forward and always the possibility of self-rescue.

Yet there is a paradox in this. We are not really separate selves at all but are deeply connected to all of life. In my truest moments, I disappear and become one with the light.

Einstein developed a formula for the relationship between energy and matter. He understood this one way, I understand it in another. Matter is our blood and bones, our loved ones, and the natural world. Energy is light, love, consciousness, and God. Beauty is all around us, boundless and timeless. All we need to do is look toward the light and we will know this.

Dear reader, you too can write your story as a life in light.

ACKNOWLEDGMENTS

Thanks to Jim, my family, friends, and the Prairie Trout, my writers' group for three decades.

And thank you to my readers: Sara Gilliam, Jane Isay, Jim Pipher, Aubrey Streit Krug, and Jan Zegers-Lens.

Thanks to Alexandra Bissell, who stepped in to help, and to Sharon Kennedy, my editorial assistant extraordinaire.

And, as always, I thank my good friend and brilliant agent of thirty years, Susan Lee Cohen.

I deeply appreciate my editor, Nancy Miller, and the great team at Bloomsbury.

I love you all.

A Life in Light: Meditations on Impermanence

Mary Pipher

The following questions are intended to enhance your discussion of *A Life in Light*.

About The Book

Throughout our lives, we will all face challenges, loss, and despair. Yet, as Mary Pipher shows in her new memoir-in-essays, we can also experience incredible beauty and deep joy. Even in times of great struggle, we can choose to focus on the things that soothe and replenish us. It is simply a matter of attention.

In *A Life in Light*, Pipher offers insight into coping with life's inevitable impermanence. Drawing on her expertise as a developmental psychologist as well as her personal experiences as a resilient child, loyal friend, young mother, orphaned daughter, and loving grandmother, she explores ways we can all cultivate light in dark times.

For Discussion

1. Mary Pipher begins the book by describing her first memory: light dancing in the leaves of a tall tree in her grandmother's front yard. She writes, "I didn't have the language, but I knew that what I was watching was beautiful." How did that experience inform her life going forward? What is your earliest memory? Is it positive or negative, and does it carry this kind of significance for you?

2. In the introduction, Pipher describes resilience as the ability to find light in dark times. "We build it by our attitudes, efforts, and coping skills." How, specifically, did Pipher's attitudes, efforts, and coping skills lead to her ability to be resilient?

3. Pipher's parents were complicated figures in her life. How did you feel about them when they were introduced in "A Motherless

Child" and "My Father's Shirt"? How did you feel about them by the end of the book?

4. When she was a child, swimming filled Pipher with a deep sense of love, safety, and well-being. What was it about swimming that generated these feelings in her?

5. In "A Best Friend," Pipher writes about the importance of friendships in childhood and says that having a best friend and confidant at age nine changed her life. How did her friendship with Jeanie change her life at this age? How did your own childhood friends help shape you and, perhaps, change your own life?

6. Pipher writes about the importance of animal companions in childhood, both wild and domesticated. What did these early encounters with animals teach her about herself, humanity, and the world?

7. Books were a solace for Pipher in her formative years. What books helped construct your identity beyond the bounds of family?

8. In "House Calls," Pipher's mom explains that parents often gave their children what they never had, not necessarily what the children wanted or needed. Have you seen this happen in your own, or someone else's, life?

9. Pipher's grandmother, her fourth-grade teacher Mrs. Oliver, and her pottery teacher Mrs. Van Cleave all made her feel truly seen. How did these adults help shape her into the woman she would become?

10. Working at the A&W taught Pipher a great deal about the world and herself. What did she learn there about people, and about work?

11. While in San Francisco with her parents, Pipher is able to see how she is both like her parents and different from them. She realizes that part of growing up and being ready to leave home is being able to accept these differences without judgment. What does she realize about her parents in this section?

12. How does Pipher react to the death of each of her parents?

13. Fame is not what Pipher wanted, but she got it anyway. What does she find challenging about it, and how does that affect her future life choices?

14. Light at different times of the day penetrates the book. Quiet dawns, bright midday sun, sunsets, and moonlight feature often. Why has light been so significant to Pipher?

15. How did the pandemic change your relationship to your home, and to the word *home*?

16. In the last section, Pipher distinguishes between ordinary happiness (which depends on the circumstances of the day) and deep happiness (which is independent of conditions). She says, "It is a matter of attention." What allowed Pipher to offer that attention? Do you agree?

17. The Japanese word *komorebi* appears throughout the book, referring to "the interplay of light and leaves as sunlight shines through trees." Pipher says that it can also "refer to a melancholic longing for a person, place, or thing that is far away. Or it can refer to impermanence. Dappled light shows us that what is here now will be gone in an instant. Nothing stays the same." How does this word deepen our understanding of impermanence? How does it relate to Pipher's feelings about resilience?

Recommended Reading:

Women Rowing North by Mary Pipher; *The Art of Living* by Thich Nhat Hanh; *When Things Fall Apart: Heart Advice for Difficult Times* by Pema Chodron; *No Time Like the Present: Finding Freedom, Love, and Joy Right Where You Are* by Jack Kornfield; *Upstream: Selected Essays* by Mary Oliver; *The Nature Fix: Why Nature Makes Us Happier, Healthier, and More Creative* by Florence Williams; *The Book of Delights* by Ross Gay; *Educated: A Memoir* by Tara Westover